ON ANYTHING

[These Essays, with one exception, first appeared in the *Morning Post* and *Morning Leader*, by courtesy of the Editors of which they are here reprinted.]

ON ANYTHING

BY

HILAIRE BELLOC

Essay Index Reprint Series

BOOKS FOR LIBRARIES PRESS
FREEPORT, NEW YORK

First Published 1910
Reprinted 1969

STANDARD BOOK NUMBER:
8369-0003-0

LIBRARY OF CONGRESS CATALOG CARD NUMBER:
79-76893

PRINTED IN THE UNITED STATES OF AMERICA

TO

GEORGE MACDONALD LEMMI

CONTENTS

Contents

ON ANYTHING

ON BUILDING CASTLES IN SPAIN

One day in the town of Perpignan I was poking about to see where I could best get something to eat, when I saw a door open into a charming garden; and in the hope of finding it to be the garden of an inn, and at any rate of seeing the garden during the process of asking whether it were an inn, I walked in, but I found everything deserted.

There was a little house at the end with everything shut against the blinding sun, but the main door of it wide open. I walked in there too and heard no noise of men, and my curiosity took me up the stairs until I came out quite unexpectedly upon another little garden built on the flat roof of this dwelling and on its shady side. And there I saw a man sitting and looking dreamily towards the mountains.

He did not ask me how I came there, but I desired to tell him, for it was evidently his roof.

We spoke a little together until I asked him why he watched the mountains and why his gaze was

B

towards Spain; then at great length he spoke to me, but dreamily still.

"Long before I knew that the speech of men was misused by them and that they lied in the hearing of the gods perpetually—in those early days through which all men have passed, during which one believes what one is told, an old and crusty woman of great wealth, to whom I was describing what I intended to do with life (which in those days seemed to me of infinite duration), said to me, 'You are building castles in Spain.' I was too much in awe of this woman—not on account of the wealth, but on account of the crust—to go further into the matter, but it seemed to me a very foolish thing to say, for I had never been to Spain, and I had nothing wherewith to build a castle—and indeed such a project had never passed through my head.

"For many years I returned to this phrase. I heard it upon several occasions. And in those years through which a man approaches maturity it still remained in my mind, possessing a singular fascination. Though I had found long since that phrases mean at the best something different from their words, and often something exactly opposite to them, yet this phrase kept about it something mystical and sincere; and I never read of Spain nor saw a map of Spain without thinking of the castles in that land, and wondering whether, as that ancient sybil had prophesied to me, I should come to build them there or no.

On Building Castles in Spain

"It so happened that the feeling grew upon me until, in my thirtieth year, I determined to travel in that country, and I did so, arriving at one of the Spanish ports by sea ; and the first thing I did when I had landed was to ask in my own tongue whether there were any castles in the neighbourhood, and especially whether any of them were at that moment in process of being built. Hearing which, the gentleman whom I had addressed bade me stay a moment where I was, upon the quay, and returned with a policeman who wore a helmet in the English manner, but whose face betrayed him. This official beckoned me to follow him ; I was closely interrogated by a member of the superior or educated classes who was also a magistrate, and after some deliberation as to whether I should not be imprisoned, I was escorted to the frontier between two armed men. Nor in the course of my journey, which was hot and uncomfortable, did I see any one building castles, so I returned as wise as I had come, but, I am glad to say, not any the poorer, for the Spanish State had taken charge of me and had paid for all that part of my journey which had taken place upon Spanish soil.

"Coming, therefore, into the Roussillon by way of the pass in the mountains, I went very sadly, but a free man, in by the Gypsies' Gate at Perpignan, and ate by myself at the Red Lion. Then, saying nothing to any one, I went over the mountains in another manner, with nothing to carry but a sack, and determined to trust only to a considerable sum

3　　　　B 2

On Anything

of money which I carried in my pocket. So I came down into Aragon, and when I got there I found it very unsuitable for the building of castles. For you must know that Aragon is almost completely composed of mud, so that any very large building, at least in the northern part, would very probably sink. Moreover, those rare rocks on which anything enduring can be founded are already occupied in that country by the priests, who have for ages forbidden the building of castles in any form, and that under the most dreadful penalties. But I found a man in Huesca who told me that, though he himself had never seen such a thing, I would no doubt find it in Saragossa, which was a capital city of enormous dimensions, and one that contained every human thing. So then I went on down the valley of the river Gallego (which was full of mud, as everything is in that district), and at last I saw before me the towers and the spires of Saragossa. But before I went into the town I thought I would first ask for information, and save myself the trouble of further walking. There was sitting with his back against a very dirty and ancient wall a man much dirtier than the wall and almost as old. Round his head was a handkerchief, and in his eyes was the stern pride of Aragon, which, though it be made out of mud, is full of courage, and breeds men who will kill you for nothing. Remembering this, and knowing that in their contempt for wealth the Aragonese will often unite good blood with poverty, I took off my hat and

4

On Building Castles in Spain

swept it about, and asked him whether his family motto were not ' *Prince ne daigne,*' to which he replied only by shaking his head in a decisive way. I then asked him whether I should find them building a castle in Saragossa, to which he said very sharply, ' No !' for the Aragonese are as terse as they are courageous. Then I said to him, ' Days, knight !' (for in this manner does one take leave in Aragon), and he replied, ' Go with God,' which is their common salutation, even to duns.

" When I had gone a little way on to the bridge which here crosses the muddy Ebro, whether there is water in the river or not, I saw a man riding on a mule who seemed to me more promising, for he was singing a song in quarter notes, which is the Spanish way. I asked him whether they were building castles in Saragossa, at which he laughed heartily, and said, ' No. Believe me, if we have any (which I doubt) it is more in our line to let them fall down than to build them.' And with these words he spoke affectionately to his mule and went his way, and I, knowing I should get no luck after such an omen, turned back and took the train into my own country."

" Did you not then," said I, " ever see building a castle in Spain ? "

" Yes," said he very sadly ; " it was in this way : there are parts of Spain which are included by mistake upon our side of the mountains, so that they have French water and forests, and one can live decently

5

there; and going in to one of these valleys upon business one day, I saw before me a very hideous thing—but there was no mistaking it: it was a castle! It was built—or rather building—of very glaring white stone; it had four turrets with very staring red tiles, half a hundred false Gothic windows, and at least twenty gargoyles, each one of which exactly resembled its neighbour, and all of which had been done by contract in Toulouse. Two statues of an offensive kind guarded the entrance to the place, and the main door of it was one of those that turn round like a turnstile so as to keep out the air; and in front of this thing was a lawn with a net. There were two trees just planted and looking as though they would rather die than live, and a little further off the workmen were digging for a fountain. It was a very saddening sight. I went up to the foreman, who by his dress seemed to be a countryman of my own, and I said, 'This is a castle that you are building, is it not?' He stared at me and said yes, wondering why I asked. 'And I think,' I went on, 'that I am in Spain, am I not?' 'Yes,' said he, wondering still more, 'the frontier lies there'—and he pointed to a little stream in the grounds. 'I thought as much,' I said, sighing profoundly. 'At last I have come upon a man building a castle in Spain.'

"Since then I have seen no other such sight, nor do I wish to see one. And ever since then I have made it my business, when I had need to build

6

On Building Castles in Spain

castles in Spain (the appetite for which comes upon me at least twice a week), to come up here on to this roof and survey the Roussillon, the Canigou and the Mediterranean Sea, and build castles in my head, for I have discovered realities to be appalling."

With these words he begged me to leave him.

ON CLAY

Let us be Antean: let us touch earth. Let us look at the pit out of which we were digged: let there be no false shame; let us talk of clay: of all the things in which the modern world has gone wrong there is nothing in which it has gone wrong more than in the point of clay. Our fathers before us, who were great men and wise—they knew what the thing was. When they had robbed a monastery or killed a king, or in some other way acquired an estate in land, what did they? They said to the steward or to the fathers of the village: "Is there no clay about?" And when they heard there was, there did they found their house. And in this way it has come about that all great Englishmen, or very nearly all great Englishmen have been born and brought up on clay.

That noble and regal city, the City of London, the second city of the West, the city which was founded by Brutus himself, the city which is directly descended from ancient Ilion and bears its glories—London, I say, could not be built save upon clay. For though at first, in their folly, the builders of London put up their wretched wattled huts on

8

On Clay

gravel, yet when the spirit took them that they would grow, and they determined to make a town of it, on to the clay they went.

Then again, the clay bred the wheat that used to grow in England, and it grew the barley also, and man, who was made of clay, lived on the clay, drank out of the burnt clay, and ate the fruit of the clay; nor is this all that clay has done for us (and what have we done for clay!), for when I speak of drinking out of the burnt clay it recalls to me another function of this admirable ungotten mineral—at least it is for the greater part ungotten. But for clay where should we be for pipkins, pannikins, porcelain of all kinds, and but for clay what should we do for the olla, for the cream jug, and for those large flat basins in which people pour milk that the cream may rise on top of it? At least the wise people, who go by the old fashions and will not use a separator—for if you know anything of the matter you will know that no pig will thrive upon skim milk unless the cream has risen from it in the old manner: and there I make an end of this digression.

You may think I have exhausted the matter of clay, but you are wrong. Clay has a further quality: it is a mystery. Any one can see how granite came about. And as for chalk, it was made by a vast number of little fishes. Sand is a thing a tom-fool can understand; limestone is self-evident; and I never knew any one yet who was puzzled by alluvial soil; but clay is a harder nut to crack. How was it

On Anything

made ? Those who were there when the foundations
of the earth were laid and who pretend that they
know everything, those whose god is matter and
whose infallible authority is printer's ink, boast
like Lucifer their father, and will explain everything to you on their eight fingers and two thumbs
—but they confess that they cannot explain clay.
It is all very well to say that clay is full of alumina ;
that it is the breaking up of granite rocks, but no
one can tell you how all this came about, nor why it
is so pasty. " It is not known " (says my Encyclopædia)
" why certain specimens of granite are rapidly cor-
roded and crumbled down, while others have resisted
for ages the same causes of decay." No ! No, by
heaven ! it is not known. And it is a great day in
modern times when one can get one of the scientists
to admit that he is not possessed of universal knowledge. No man living knows how clay came to be.
I repeat it is a mystery and is crammed with the
virtue of all mysterious things. And should it not
be mysterious, seeing what are its powers ?

For remember that all this does but touch upon
the edge and fringe of the greatness of clay. Records were first kept in clay, and but for clay would
never have survived. They were scratched on clay
tablets and burnt, and they have come down to our
own time. Bricks have to be made from clay, and
with bricks did men first learn to build small and
reasonable houses, for before they thought of bricks
the rich man could live in stone, but the poor man

On Clay

had to do as best he could in wood and wattles. But the moment they thought of clay and of making bricks, reasonable houses for the middle-class appeared ; and with the middle-class there came also public opinion, common-sense, good manners, verse, sculpture, and the art of living.

You may very reasonably prove, and to the satisfaction of most men, that without clay there could be no middle-class ; nor does this great service which the clay has done us by any means exhaust the debt we owe to clay. There would be no dew ponds on the chalk heights of England had not our ancestors long before history carefully puddled clay. And very probably there would be no statues in the world had it not been for clay, for it is clay that suggests the statue. So whenever you see a good statue (of which there are so many in this world, as for instance : the Madonna over the south porch of Rheims ; the Mary Magdalen at Brou ; the statue of Our Lady of Paris in Notre Dame ; the Venus of Milo, which is by no means the first-comer among statues ; the headless Victory with wings, which is a first-rate statue and looks as if it was going to fly down the steps of the Louvre ; the statue of the archer in that same gallery ; the statue of St. John the Baptist in South Kensington, which is a copy of the one in the Luxembourg—or indeed of any other statue)—I say, when you see a statue that is good and pleases you, remember clay. But for clay that statue could never have been.

On Anything

Do you think that with this we have come to the end of what clay has done? Why, we have not, so to speak, begun the first page of the volume!

But for clay there would be no smoking: clay made pipes. And but for clay we should not be able to drain our fields. From clay also comes aluminium, which has some purpose or other, I forget what; and clay made the Sologne. For that great heath and desert, which so few men know, owes its very life to clay. It is the clay holding the water which has turned it into the forest it is, full of little pools and cram full of wild boars and other ingenious beasts.

Roses adore the clay—they are as native to clay as salt is to the sea; and there is another thing we owe to clay, for if we had no clay we should have no roses; and talking of that, the oak is a clay tree. All that gnarled, hard, native stuff which you clap your hand on when you strike an oak beam is nourished and made strong by clay. An oak may be called the living son of the dead clay; it is a sort of clay turned vegetable, a slow, a fundamental, and an enduring thing.

Now by way of ending! Being a modern man, you will grumble and say, " Yes, but it is bad to live on." You are wrong. It is the best soil of any to live on. True, if you are a town man you find that your feet get wet on it; you cannot walk about after a shower as you can in London; therefore you prefer to be upon gravel or sand. That is because you are

On Clay

artificial and a snob.   You were intended, my lamb,
to plunge about in mud when the weather is muddy—
it is an excellent discipline for the soul.   And all
that love of sand and gravel goes with rhododendrons,
copper beeches, and villas of red brick, and the death
of the soul.   You will then object that the house
built upon clay goes up and down, heaving, as it were,
with the weather.   Why not?   All things that live
and are worthy have in themselves the principle of
motion.   Would you inhabit something dead?
Aristotle has said it, that death, the absence of life,
is essentially rigidity, the absence of motion.   Give
thanks then that your house should shift, and that
the water that you must drink on clay is of a muddy
kind ; it is better for your health than that sparkling
stuff which gives men goitre in the high hills.

In a word, there is nothing human nor anything
about man which is not the better for clay.   He
was made of clay, he should live on clay, his wood
must be the fruit of clay, and so must his food, and
so must his drink, and so must the flowers that are
his ornament.   And when he dies the very best soil
in which you can bury him is clay.

13

ON NO BOOK

AND ITS ADVANTAGES AS A COMPANION
TO TRAVEL

I KNOW very well that there are men going about who will pretend that when a thing is not there it may be neglected, and that existence is the only thing that counts, but these are ignorant and common men who have not read the philosophers of North Germany, and in particular the divine Hegel. For to us who live upon the summit of human thought it is manifest that there is no such thing as nothing, and that the absence of a thing or the non-existence of a thing is but another aspect of its presence or its existence. So Bergmann (I translate him into Latin, for German is a difficult tongue) "*esse antequam non esse esse satis constat.*" So also Biggs, his greatest living pupil at Oxford, "The moment we grant potentiality to entity——" Hold!

What I am driving at, good people, is that a man who takes no book upon a holiday forms very worthily one of the series of men who do, and I will confess that this No Book is the book I invariably

14

On No Book

take with me, in every distant journey which those
who meet me upon them may think holidays, but
which I myself have always considered to be occupation and life.

Its many advantages! . . . . Up in Bigorre,
branching northward from the main Roman Road
across the Pyrenees, runs a torrent which falls in
perhaps a thousand falls from the height and the
mountains, and whose valley forms a very difficult
approach to Spain. Now if a man be cut off by this
torrent, rising after fresh rain and threatening his
life, and if he attempts to ford it, what book do you
think would survive? So the Peña Blanca; it is not
a rock for mountaineers, but for true travelling men.
Your mountaineer, your Alpine Club mountaineer,
travels with a bath, a tent, and in general a baggage
train; he can carry books if he likes; he climbs with
a weight on his back or compels a servant to do so,
but no man can get down the Peña Blanca or up it
on the steep side with a Liddell and Scott or a
London Directory on his back. There are places on
Peña Blanca where everything you brought with you,
including your boots, you wish were away, and these
places are places where the body is in the shape of
an X, the right foot, the left foot, the right hand and
the left hand each trying to persuade itself that it
has a hold, and the co-ordinating spirit within also
asserting by sheer faith that the surface of the rock
does not lean outwards. What would a man do with
a book in such a place as this?—I mean with a book

15

in its aspect of existence ? No Book is worth more than a whole library to a man so placed and so thinking.

Consider the sea. There is only room to cook forward on condition the hatch is up ; aft, the other men are playing cards. Then again, it is either calm or rough. If it is calm the boat sways intolerably and everything reminds you of oil. What book can suit that mood ? And when, contrariwise, the boat is taking it green every few seconds, and your eyes are bleared trying to see through the spindrift and the snow, what would you do with a book—is there any book in the world that would help you to drive her through ? Are there oilskins for books ?

The horse also : for whether a rich man has lent you one, or whether it is your own, or whether it is one you have hired (and this sort go lame), the horse enters into every bit of travel. Who will read a book where a horse is concerned ? Indeed I have often considered that men who will learn everything from books and go into court or throw the family fortune into chancery on the strength of " The Pocket Lawyer " ; all men who will build a boat after instructions printed upon paper and then wonder where they have failed ; all men who consider life from printed things, would be the better for receiving, closely reading, annotating and thoroughly mastering a volume called " The Horse and How to Ride Him." It is a large flat book with diagrams, something like an atlas in shape and weight. This, I say, when they have mastered it, let them take under the right arm, holding it as a bird would hold a thing under its wing, and so accoutred let them climb upon a mustang, and digging those enormous Mexican spurs which are the glory of the West deep and hard into the brute's hide, they will discover as in a lightning flash of revelation the value of books in the large concerns of life. No Book is the book for all the plains between the Sangre de Cristo and the Sierras.

The same is true of the desert, though why I cannot tell, unless it be that by day it is too hot, and by night there is nothing to read by. Soldiers— real soldiers I mean—carry no books until they have reached the grade of general officer ; and what books do you think were regretfully laid down when the *Brunswick* went into action on the first of June, 1794 ?

I can indeed consider no active occupation for a man in which No Book is not a true companion, and that book shall be my companion in future, as it has been in the past, all over the world.

ON IRONY

Irony is that form of jest in which we ridicule a second person in the presence of a third. It is most complete when the second person is most ignorant of our intention, the third person most alive to it. Irony exists and is full even when the second person thus attacked is alone in suffering the attack, and irony exists and is full when the third person is restricted to our own expectant selves or even to God who made us and in whom is mirrored the universal truth of things. Irony enjoys an exuberant life, whether the second person so attacked is universal and the third as restricted as can be ; or whether the second person so attacked is particular and singular, and the third person, the onlooker and the audience, comprehends the whole world.

It is in the intention of irony that it should do good, because it is of the nature of irony that it should avenge the truth. I say "avenge" because irony would not be irony were it not destined to inflict a fatal, or at least a grievous, wound. There is not in irony any measure of pity for the enemy, though irony could not exist without some vast

On Irony

motive of pity for a victim in whose defence it was aroused. Irony is a sword, and must be used as a sword. It has this quality about it, that, like some faery sword, it cannot be used with any propriety save in God's purpose; and those who have been the most expert swordsmen, when they take a wrong reward for their service, or use that weapon for an unworthy end, find it fail in their hands. Nay, like any faery sword, in hands that use it unworthily it will disappear. And the history of Letters is full of men who, tempted by this or by that, by money or by ease, or by random friendship, or by some appetite lower than the hunger and thirst after justice, have found their old strong irony grow limp and fruitless after they had sold their souls.

Irony, therefore, is unknown in those societies where the love of ease dominates all men. It is most powerful in those societies which are by their temper military. You will find irony treated angrily, as though it were an acid or a poison, where men love ease. And you will find it merely ignored when men have wholly lost the sense of justice. In such societies it retires from the realm of letters to that more powerful sphere in which divine vengeance and divine necessity have their action over things; and many such a society no longer capable of producing or of appreciating irony when it proceeds from the mouth or the pen of a man, learn it most dreadfully in the catastrophes of war.

On Anything

To the young, the pure, and the ingenuous, irony must always appear to have in it a quality of something evil, and so it has, for, as I have said, it is a sword to wound. It is so directly the product or reflex of evil that, though it can never be used, nay, can hardly exist, save in the chastisement of evil, yet irony always carries with it some reflections of the bad spirit against which it was directed. How false it is to say that vengeance and the hatred of the evil men are in themselves evil, all human history can prove. Nay, but for irony in the last times of a decline no breath of health would remain to man. Nevertheless, as it is called into being by evil things, it works in an evil light. It suggests most powerfully the evil against which it is directed, and those innocent of evil shun so terrible an instrument.

Alone of the powers of expression possessed by the human spirit wherewith to defend right against wrong, irony is invulnerable, and alone of those powers it can always strike. Nor is anything invulnerable against it save that death of the intelligence which comes so shortly before the death of the society suffering it, that there is no need in the interval to attack the evil of that society or to attempt to remedy it; for when stupidity comes upon a State all is over.

A happy world, such as the world of children, or any society of men who have still preserved the general health of the soul, such a society as may be found in many mountain valleys, needs none of this salt for the curing and the preservation of morals. But even where men have so protected primal virtue, old men, old proverbs, dim records of past misfortunes leave some savour of irony in the traditions of the tribe.   And irony is proved native to the scheme of things and not of its own self unnatural or rebellious by the manner in which the mere course of human happenings is perpetually filled with it.   A dreadful irony is present when a man, having heard of the death of a friend, receives later his living letter posted from far off before that death.   There is irony when, every defence having been made against some natural accident, that accident yet enters by another gate unsuspected to man.   There is an irony in every unfulfilled prophecy and in every lengthy and worthless calculation.   No man having purchased an honour defends unpurchased honour without the spirit of irony surrounding all his words. No man praises courage being himself but a rhetorician, or praises justice being himself a lawyer or a magistrate, without some savour of irony in the air of his audience, and it may be presumed without too much phantasy that spirits equal and undisturbed and of a high intelligence can see in every action of human life save the most holy an irony as strong as that which inhabits the tragedies of the great poets.

There is a last use for irony, or rather a last aspect of it which this general irony of Nature, and of Nature's God, suggests : I mean that irony which can only appear in the letters of a country when

On Anything

corruption has gone so far that the mere truth is vivid with ironical power.

For there comes a time—it is brief, as must be all final moments of decay—but there comes a time in the moral disruption of a State when the mere utterance of a plain truth laboriously concealed by hypocrisy, denied by contemporary falsehood, and forgotten in the moral lethargy of the populace, takes upon itself an ironical quality more powerful than any elaboration of special ironies could have taken in the past. Some truth too widely put aside and quietly thrust forward, a detail in general conversation about a powerful man strikes, in such societies, exactly like the point of a spear. Blood flows : and the blood is drawn by irony. Yet was here no act nor any fabric of words. Mere testimony to the truth was enough : and this should prove that irony is in touch with the divine and is a minister to truth. In such awful moments in the history of a State that which makes the dreadful jest is not the jester, but the eternal principle of truth itself. That which is jested at is the whole texture of the universal society upon which the truth falls, and for the audience, for the third person who shall see the jest at the second person's expense, there is present nothing less than the power by which truth is of such effect among men.

No man possessed of irony and using it has lived happily ; nor has any man possessing it and using it died without having done great good to his fellows and secured a singular advantage to his own soul.

ON THE SIMPLICITY OF WORDS

THAT is simple which, when you have long looked at it, and when you have carefully considered it, you cannot justly discover to be built up of other unities. That is simple which, when we will divide it, divides into things like itself, and which, when we divide it, divides, not of its own nature, but violently and unnaturally by our volition. The acute mind will divide what is simple as freely as it will divide what is complex, but the just mind recognises simplicity and will not attempt its division. For in all analysis it is the business of the analyser to get at the ultimate unities; when he has reached the ultimate unities it is also his business to respect them: further division will show acuteness, but it will not show judgment.

The simplest thing we know is the soul of man, for it has about it a quality as it were crystalline and one. So that the more fundamentally it does a thing the more that thing is one. The powers of the soul, its instruments, and therefore the parts of its machinery, are innumerable and perhaps infinite (for we are said to be made in the image of the Infinite); but the thing itself is utterly simple.

Now the soul of man impresses, receives and expresses certain things : for instance, it impresses its unity upon things outside of it, it talks of " London," " mankind," " this landscape." It receives and it says of a colour, " This is such and such a colour " ; of a tone, " This is such and such a tone " ; of a truth hitherto unheard, " This is true—this is consonant with my nature, and with my making (for I was made); this has Authority, for Authority is authorship."

The soul of man impresses, receives and expresses. And, note you, in this business the soul of man has designed an instrument, and this instrument is the Word. Those who question whether the soul of man so acts, can only question from one of two causes : either they have not considered how we think and do, or else, like many men in our modern diliquescence, they believe all knowledge to be equally futile, and they despair equally of all kinds of careful view, whether of things that can be handled or of immaterial things.

The soul of man impresses, receives and expresses, and its instrument is the Word. It impresses its unity upon this mass of houses and people (" houses " and " people " are themselves words), and it stamps that impression as a word : " London." The soul of man receives. A certain physical impression (which a modern theory would have depend upon proportionate undulation—but this, like most physical hypotheses, is not proved) stirs in the mind a sentiment of colour and of a certain colour; and the mind records its reception in a word: blue. The soul of man expresses. It is cognisant and, in its own manner, sure of existence, secure in existence. To express this, to put forward its certainty exteriorly, out of itself, its instrument is again a word. It says, "I am."

Well then, the Word is all-important, for without the Word the soul of man would live within itself, and therefore stand imprisoned and null, a sort of death. And the Word is all-important in a second way, for by the Word the soul of man not only lives but also communicates. It is by the Word that soul and soul recognise, fertilise and enrich among themselves, each all its fellows. But there is a third character of dignity attaching to the Word, which is this: that the Word reflects and carries on, inherits, shows forth in little, presents, that great origin the soul of man, whence it proceeded; and here it is that I come to the kernel of my subject.

For it is my business to argue here that there is a mystical quality—that is, a quality not contradictory of reason but superior to it—inhabiting the right use of Words. I would say more: I would say that upon the exactitude of that quality in use depended the magic of the poets.

Very certainly men at random, any men, may experience the unexpressed emotion, but the

On Anything

function of the poet—in which he is a sort of splendid servant—is to bring words to his master, his fellow-man, the innumerable, and to untie his tongue.

Two things are most noticeable in this character of the poet: first, that he has the capacity to put these words before his fellow-men for their use, and of the right sort and in the right order ; and secondly, that neither does he know how he does it nor can mortal man in any place or under any influence explain how it is done. Consider these three lines—

Πέμπε δὲ μιν πομποῖσιν ἅμα κραιπνοῖσι φέρεσθαι
Ὕπνῳ καὶ Θανάτῳ διδυμάοσιν· οἵ ῥά μεν ὦκα
Κάτθεσαν ἐν Λυκίης εὐρείης πίονι δήμῳ.

Let us suppose this translated by some man who would put an English word for nearly every Greek word, not considering that such mere transformation was by no means a resurrection of the dead. It is from the *Iliad*, where the body of Sarpedon is ordered by a god to be taken to Lycia—to which place he belonged. This god orders the body of Sarpedon, fallen in battle, to be taken to his native place ; and this is how the poet speaks of his transference from the place where he died to his own land, if you put word for word—

"He gave him to be borne at once by swift companions, the twins Sleep and Death, who swiftly laid him in the rich land of Lycia the full."

Now a man caring more for resurrection than for a

26

On the Simplicity of Words

mechanical transference might put it in many ways—I suggest this—

" And he gave Sarpedon dead to be borne by swift companions, the twin-Gods Sleep and Death, who bore him to his own land of Lycia, a pleasant land."

I care not how it is translated, for whoever translates it, unless he is inspired (that is, ordered from outside mankind by a spirit), he will translate it wrong. But the nearer we get to the violent truth of those famous words the more we see what the Word is to the Soul, the more we see how the simplicity of the Word reflects and, to our eyes (and our ears), in some way enhances the simplicity of the Soul.

These toppling things which a man can neither escape nor avoid reside (it would seem from such a passage) not only in the inmost soul but also in Words. These words once written, the soul that put them forth has done its work for ever. Yet no man can say that common counters have been used, that a mere currency of expression has here done its work.

What could be more worn, what for all time more common, than these considerations, a dead man, companions, home, death, sleep and a fertile valley ? But in some way it is possible to make of these things what was there made when the man who so wrote them wrote them ; and there is no one who will not feel that a son of the gods, of the high gods, was taken by lesser but divine servants, Death and Sleep,

27

On Anything

who brought him back dead to where his mother had
borne him, the land of Lycia, a pleasant land ; and
he was so borne out of battle, and he rested when
the fight was done.

Now how is that purpose of words achieved?
No man knows. No man can explain : it is the
power of the Word, it is the magic power of the
Word. There are some (poor fools !) who try to
analyse the connotation of the Word ; they will show
how such and such a Word involving (in such and
such a civilisation) such memories and such associa-
tions plays a trick with the mind and deceives it.
They will show how Elizabethan English stirs us by
modern experiences which the words used by the
Elizabethans recall. But the whole of their philosophy is upset at once by the consideration of such a
passage as this which I have quoted ; for here are
only the simplest of things, as simple, I say, as the
human soul, and at once overwhelming.

There is more to be said than the mere praise of
so amazing a success ; the right choice of words in
this example, or (to speak more accurately) the right
acceptation of them—for poets do not choose—does
much more than merely *say* that thing which such
words should say. It does much more than only *tell*
what the singer was inspired to tell. It expands,
and embranches and conceives. And out of the
right acceptation of words there grows a sacred and a
further explanation of their meaning : they illumine
not only what we are but what we might be and

28

On the Simplicity of Words

what we will be. And, above all, they raise echoes : they raise echoes from beyond the world.

Thus in that little bit of Homer quoted, do you not see what it means beyond its bare poetic statement ? Not only did Death and Sleep take the body of Sarpedon back to Lycia, but the bodies of all of us are in such hands : for (if you will think of it closely) in what way do men recover their innocence, their childhood and the place where they were born ? In what way do they pierce through time ? By sleep, in dreams, and possibly, in a more final manner, by death.

ON SECLUDED PLACES

It is a commonplace, and a true one, that the modern world is full of illusions, or rather that the things which we interest ourselves about to-day are nearly all of them matters upon which we have no direct knowledge. The climate of Jamaica, a foreign trial, a war between two nations neither of which we have visited, come to entertain us far more than things upon which we have immediate and personal experience. After a little while we come also to judge these things as though we knew them.

I say that the whole modern world (with the exception of the peasants) suffers heavily from this disease, and no one more than politicians and their electorate. Of a politician upon whose judgment may depend the happiness of the country, most of those who admire or hate him have an impression drawn from caricatures. Of the electorate whom they are supposed to serve politicians have a vague conception, drawn from the hurried aspect of vast crowds of poor men seen by gaslight after dinner in huge halls, and in the course of all the distractions of a speech.

This fantastic ignorance which modern conditions

On Secluded Places

have bred in the great towns seems to some to be
wholly evil in its effect. It is not so ; for among its
effects are to be discovered a number of joyful
surprises. Many things which we had imagined to
be such and such and which we had deplored, turned
out upon examination to be very different, and much
better than our newspaper picture had conceived.
Among these joyful surprises is the discovery that
the earth is not full, that travel has not overspread
it, and that there is perfect loneliness within the
reach of all. No popular conception of the modern
world is more firmly held, especially by educated,
and therefore by jaded, men. There is none which
it is more useful to explode. Two things have come
side by side : first, an immense increase in the ease of
communications ; secondly, a positive delight in the
crowd to associate with the crowd ; and these two
facts, the one economic and the other social, have
more than counteracted all the expansion in numbers
of those who travel about and defile the earth with
their presence. In between the tracks of their
travel, a few miles upon the centres in which they
herd, pig and pen, there is an isolation which our
forefathers never knew. A hundred years ago the
Land's End and St. Davids were both places far
removed from London ; to-day the end of Cornwall
is familiar to many thousands of men who are not
native to it, but what about St. Davids ? How many
men who read this can say where it is or have visited
it ? A hundred years ago Midhurst, Petworth,

31

On Anything

Pulborough, Horsham, East Grinstead, Crowborough Top, Haywards Heath, Heathfield, Burwash, were places upon the map of Sussex intimately known to the men of that county, and visited but rarely by men from beyond the weald. But though they were visited rarely they were visited equally, and if a man said he knew the county then he knew those places. Compare their fate to-day. Crowborough, Haywards Heath, and Heathfield are suburbs of London, and right through the heart of the county a long bridge —pure London all the way—unites London with its suburb of Brighton. Do you imagine upon that account that the isolation of Sussex is lost? Very far from it. It is considerably increased. Nay, the loneliness of that vast proportion of the county which lines of travel do not touch is, if anything, too great—it is in excess even of what the greatest lover of contemplation can desire. And you may within a mile of the Brighton road lie in a wood and watch small beasts behaving with a freedom and an ignorance of human intercourse which perhaps they never had when village life was really strong, when the great estates were not mortgaged to cosmopolitan finance, when the old families lived in their houses and made the county town five miles away their resort for purchase and even for amusement.

It is equally true of the North; the whole chain of the Pennines between the two main lines of travel to the east and to the west of them is utterly deserted. A man may walk thirty times in a year

On Secluded Places

from Hawes to Ribble Head and in not half those walks meet or speak to a man. This is true of the great high road across the chain, of the summits it is far truer. Go from Appleby over Cross Fell up Wild Boar Scar and down the water to Alston, and you will be as completely cut off from men the whole day long as you could be in the West of Canada. The same is true of the dales of Cheviot. From where Chevy Chase was fought all the way up Rededale is a fine great road that was once the highway to Scotland over Carter Fell. If a man goes lame upon the English side of it he cannot count upon getting a lift to Jedburgh; he must limp it all the way. And speaking of that road reminds one that not only has this novel isolation come upon a great part of Britain, but that as one watches it with a sense that is not wholly pleasurable (especially on winter evenings, after a day bereft of human intercourse) one has often around one evidences of a recent time when the activities of the country were more evenly spread. Upon this same great road from Carter Fell there is upon the Scotch side of the path a house which once paid a high rental and did great trade with the traffic. It is in ruins. Upon that same Cross Fell which is now completely alone, you come perpetually upon abandoned workings, upon bits of hardened road, now half sunk into the bog, and even upon the remains of broken bridges over streams.

In the quadrilateral which is formed by the railways in the south-west of Scotland there is a great area of silence, and in that belt of Wales which separates the northern from the southern dialects a belt which is again served by a fine high road, and which has been throughout English history the scene of the western advance from across the Marches into the Principality, there is silence also. Plinlimmon, the mountain which dominates this central part, is unknown, and the reason is easy enough to discover. Plinlimmon is not an abrupt mountain, astonishing in outline or difficult of ascent. It is, upon the contrary, a great rounded hill, but there is perhaps no height in the island more solemn nor commanding a more awful and spacious scene, and those few who would still take the trouble to reach it may find the north a chasm more wonderful, I think, than any in the range of Snowdon or in the neighbourhood of Cader Idris. All this is true of that little narrow space which lies between the North Sea and St. George's Channel, and when one considers the neighbouring countries of the Continent the instances that arise are innumerable. Within two days of London, and to be reached at about an expense of £2, there is a little democracy in which no man has ever been put to death, in which no wheeled vehicles have ever been seen, of which the few laws are made, or rather the ancient and honourable customs maintained, by the heads of families meeting for discussion. You can from the little village in its centre telephone to Paris if you wish, and yet who has been to that place? Or who knows the way there from London?

On Secluded Places

Probably not a dozen men.   There is on one of the main railways of Europe a chain of mountains abrupt, intensely blue, comparable only to the background of certain mediæval illuminations, and, with their astonishing, unworldly aspect, making one understand how the active mediæval imagination could see, remember, and use things that we pass by.   I know of no artist who has drawn that range nor of any traveller who has described it.   You cannot see it from the train; it runs along a narrow and profound valley.   You must leave the railway at a little roadside station, you must climb two thousand feet on to the plateau above, and from there, when you have turned a corner of the road, there breaks upon you this unearthly vision of the range.

Now consider that example—and it will not be difficult to discover how and why these places remain, or rather increasingly become, isolated from the modern world.   For what must you do to obtain a view of what I have spoken? You must abandon the express, with its speed and luxury, to which you are accustomed; you must get into a little slow and dingy local train, you must climb a high hill in spite of weather.   You may do it once from curiosity, but you are not compelled to the open air and the road as were your fathers, and for one man that will rarely be at the pains to go about to visit and to understand the world there are a thousand who would rather delude themselves into a *simulacrum* of the emotions of travel by reading of them in some book, and that

On Anything

book will probably have been written by some one
who has no more followed the road than themselves.
For a man to know the world he must not sleep
now and again in the open, or now and again for
a freak in some dirty inn where there is bad
cooking and bad wine ; he must so sleep continually
day after day. He must not have only an object
before him in his journey, such as the visiting of a
famous shrine ; he must also have an object all the
way along, to note whatever he may pass; and he
must so draw his itinerary that it shall be something
out of the common, that is, something exposing one
always to discomfort and often to peril. There are
few men who care to pay the price, and, after all, the
effect of their hesitation is excellent, for they run off
to vulgarise the New World and the Far East, and
they leave England and Europe to the intimacy of
those who love them best.

ON PEOPLE IN BOOKS

It is a matter for the curious to examine (but not the wisest will determine it) why people in books are so extraordinarily different from real people. You might imagine that the people in biographies at least would be more or less like human beings—but they never are. A man may say that the reason of this is that biography to-day is always a sort of modern, pale, conventional, and hypocritical affair—that the biographer dare not print nine-tenths of his material under our modern tyranny of suppression, and that he has necessarily to make a puppet of his man. But there are others besides modern biographies, and it is true of them all that the people inside are not human. You have biographies of politicians acting upon principle ; biographies of men who have accumulated vast fortunes without a hint of their main passion ; biographies of men of lineage in which you are given to understand that their distinction was due to some individual worth and force. Biographies of the frankest and most brutal periods, biographies of men long dead, biographies written by enemies, all have this in common, that the person inside the book does not go on like a human being.

On Anything

Autobiographies give one a better chance, but even there, though you get something much more vivid, you never get a real man. It seems as though the writing of an autobiography or confession always went with a twist, either morbid or megalomaniac. Take the very best one of all, Rousseau's; it can be proved, and research has proved it, that he is perpetually maligning himself. As for St. Augustine's (oh, how dull!) he tells us so little, and his purpose is so far from being autobiographical that it does not come under the same criticism; and as for Borrow, those who have read him assure me that he is perpetually performing marvellous feats of intelligence and courage to which there is no witness at all but himself. Hagiographers are appalling. They do not attempt to present a living figure, though I will make an exception for one account of the death of St. Thomas of Canterbury; I forget which, but it is full of realities. Your stock hagiographer, as, for instance, he of the Carolingian period, postulates three things: the noble birth of his hero, his boldly standing up to somebody else (usually a layman), and his performing a number of actions precisely similar to those which others of the type have performed; it is almost mechanical; it is like the leader in a party newspaper describing a party speech by a party man.

People in histories also are not human beings. The moment you try to make them human in writing your history a demon enters and makes you make a

On People in Books

great quantity of little mistakes. For instance, you are writing about a man with one eye, and you are determined to make him human ; you find out all you can about that eye, whether the other one was of glass, or was just left screwed up in the old-fashioned style. You get right about the date of the time when he lost his eye, the effect which his one eye had on other people, and all the rest of it. You make the man live again before you, and the moment you begin writing about him you will make his left eye his right eye. It is the knowledge of this, and the fear of the powerful Demon who works it, that makes historians shun the human being and stuff their books full of ghosts paler than any that wander by Acheron.

This is especially true of historians of war. The people they write about occupy " strategic " points (a phrase which is blankly meaningless to the writer as to the reader), they " grasp " the situation at a glance, they " master detail," they are (when the author is against them), " in spite of all their faults, not devoid of physical courage," or (if the author is in favour of them) " acting with that quiet decision which is characteristic of them " (and of bad actors in problem plays, too, by the way), but they never live.

Now and then you get flashes ; the eyes glance, the tones take on reality, there is a human voice and gesture, but it dies again. Perhaps the most vivid and most fascinating of such histories in our tongue

On Anything

is Napier's. You will continually find such flashes in it—but they are not permanently connected. It is odd that the most living of histories are the exceedingly simple and bald relations set down under primitive conditions of society when a man merely desired to chronicle dates and facts. How it is so no one can tell, but a plain statement of some not very interesting thing with just a verb and a substantive will do the trick. For instance, where Eginhard says of Charlemagne that everything about him was virile "except his voice, which was high," or again, where Fulcher of Chartres (I think it is) says of a spy on the crusading march that he was "short in the nose and in every virtue." But even the early historians build up no continuously living figure.

When it comes to novelists the matter is notorious. The people in novels not only do not go on like real people, but they do things sometimes physically, always morally, impossible to real people. I have often wished to know a professional novelist in order to ask him why his people went on like that. To take quite small points. A lover and his lady in a novel will often hunt the fox. So far so good. There is nothing impossible about that. When they have done running after the animal they go home together, and their horses walk side by side. How is that done? Except horses in cavalry regiments or in circuses, or horses constrained and tied by leather thongs in front of wheeled vehicles, when were two horses ever seen that walked the same

On People in Books

pace side by side? The novelist may say that it is
necessary to the convention of his novel. It would
spoil a love scene if he showed one of the two horses
dragging further and further behind the other (as
one of them always does), and then having to canter
or trot every three minutes to catch up his neighbour,
and it would also spoil his love scene if he made one
of the horses walking slowly and the other dancing,
which in real life is one of the ways in which people
attempt to keep two horses abreast. But there are
many things in your novel which have no such
excuse, and which are equally out of Nature. For
instance, people sit down suddenly and write enormous cheques at a moment's notice. Now even the
richest man cannot do that. He has his money
invested, he does not waste it by letting it lie idle in
gigantic balances of a current account. Then again,
the things they do with their mouths. " ' No,' she
laughed." How on earth could that be done? If
you try to laugh and say " No " at the same time it
sounds like neighing—yet people are perpetually
doing it in novels. If they did it in real life they
would be locked up. Another thing that people do
in novels on all sides is to make immensely long
speeches. Sometimes the whole of the author's
views upon some big matter, like the fate of the
soul for instance, comes pouring out in a solid page
and a half of spoken stuff. In real life the only
people who do this are politicians, and even they only
do it on stated and ritual occasions; they do not do it

in private houses. Sometimes they try, but they are interrupted.

Yet again, consider the vast number of titles which people have in novels. I cannot call to mind one single novel without a title—I mean no novel of the modern kind. Of course there must be such, but they are certainly rare. Now in real life things are not thus. All the ordinary people of this country go about day after day without meeting lords and ladies, but in novels something like half the characters come in quite casually with titles, and I have been told that it is a matter of professional pride with some novelists to be able to get the complicated system of English titles exactly right, and that they will even fabricate difficult problems for the pleasure of solving them, as do men who play chess. They will take the younger son of an earl, make him a Colonial Cabinet Minister, and then triumphantly settle for you which of the two "honourables" he is; or again, they will marry the heiress of a marquisate inheritable in the female line to the eldest son of a man who comes into a barony later on in the book—and get it absolute. But people in real life do not care much about these things.

Conversely, a very large number of things that *do* happen in real life and are interesting never seem to get into novels. For instance, repetitions. Your hero will fall off a horse and break something, but he does not do it twenty times as he would if he were a

On People in Books

living being.   A man comes late to dinner, but he is not always coming late to dinner as he would if he were human : and, what is worse, a score of highly interesting real types never get between covers at all.

Take, for instance, that immoderately common type, among the most common of God's creatures, which I will call " the Silent Fool," the man who hardly ever talks, and when he does says something so overwhelmingly silly that one remembers it all one's life.   I can recollect but one Silent Fool in modern letters, but he comes in a book which is one of the half-dozen immortal achievements of our time, a book like a decisive battle, or like the statue of John the Baptist at South Kensington, a glory for us all.   I mean *The Diary of a Nobody*.   In that you will find the silent Mr. Padge, who says " That's right "—and nothing more.

One might go on for ever piling up instances of this divorce between the supposed pictures of our modern life and the truths of it.   I will end with what is to me, perhaps, the most glaring of all : the attitude of fiction towards what is called " success." No matter who the author is, no matter what his knowledge of the world, he simply cannot draw " successful men " as they are, that is, in a diversity as great as any to be discovered in the human race. Men who have "got on," that is, who are at once well to do and well known, are as different as men with the toothache or as men with warts on their chins.

43

On Anything

Some are kind, some brutal, some clever, some
stupid, some got their money by luck, some by
inheritance, some by theft, some few by being able
to make or do something better than their fellows,
but at any rate in real life, when you are about to
meet some one who is known to you as " successful,"
you never have the slightest idea what you are going
to meet, your last experience of the sort is no guide
to the next, and the " successful " chap may turn out
to be anything at all. But in novels your wealthy
and well-known man is invariably powerful in
character. It never fails. He may be good or bad,
English or foreign, young or old, but he always has in
him something of what you see in a very good sergeant-
major at a few shillings a week, an experienced head
master at a few hundreds a year, or a capable
engineer on a passenger ship. He displays qualities
which have no more to do with what is called
" success " now-a-days than red hair or brown boots
have. In a word, your successful man is a type in
the novel. In real life he is not a type at all—he is
any one. And another thing you never get in a
novel is a well-mannered man or a bad-mannered
man. I cannot recollect one character who inter-
rupts at the top of his voice, nor one who joins the
conversation of others in an easy way. . . . But
suppose one filled a novel with real people, what
escape would there be from daily life ?

ON THE EFFECT OF TIME

Of all contrasts the most ironical and the most profound is the contrast between the Tag and the Truth of the Tag. A couple of lines are chosen by humanity from the work of a great poet, and are usually so chosen not only because they are beautiful, but because they are true. When they have been repeated a certain number of times they become a tag. A proverb or a mere popular statement puts into the shortest possible form some extremely simple, and perhaps extremely obvious, at any rate (this is quite certain) some extremely important, truth. Every one sees it is a truth, everybody repeats it, and it becomes a tag.

Now note the next phase in the life of the said tag. It is criticised and it is ridiculed; it becomes a solid butt for the archery of human wit. That phase lasts, perhaps, the lifetime of a man.

Now note the third phase, for it will teach you the most that can be learnt about mankind, and it is endless. It is the consummation of the tag and the test of humanity afforded by the tag. The tag is now taken for granted and is eternal, and the following things happen to it : children are taught it like the alphabet; they are compelled to learn it. Hobbledehoys, great wits, and leaders of thought avoid it because it is commonplace. They can be seen waggling from one side of the road to the other in their grotesque efforts to avoid the tag. The whole world knows that the tag is there. Lastly—most wonderful of all !—the tag ceases to bite : it ceases to affect men; men are saturated with it. Men are acclimatised to it. They are vaccinated with it; and the tag has now arrived at the exercise of its eternal function, which is to wake in individuals, here in one man, there in another, an overwhelming sense of its truth (or beauty). It begins its career of converting individual men. Let it be mentioned where three are gathered together, and it will be fled from as an out-used thing, but two can make confidences each to the other about it, and one can feel it like a thorn or like a gem in his heart.

"Who goes a-borrowing goes a-sorrowing" has gone through all these phases; so has "Waste not want not." So has "For who to dull forgetfulness a prey," etc. So has "Felix qui potuit," etc. And so have the three or four thousand others that are the stock of a proper mind.

All these set me thinking of yet another tag, and as it is that which most sharply tests humility and, through humility, intelligence, and as, therefore, in this not very humble and not intelligent time it is grossly neglected, there is a pleasure in dwelling

On the Effect of Time

upon it. It is to this effect : " The future is veiled from man."

Good Lord ! To read the Press and to hear the speeches ! Why, one would think that the future had a map to it ! One can hardly hear one's self think for prophecies ; and, what is perhaps the most terrible thing of all, as a symptom of our modern state of mind, the prophecies have a dogmatic quality (using the word " dogmatic " as it is popularly used of transcendental affirmations), for men prophesy in great herds and all together, and to question their prophecies, simply to say that possibly " the future *is* veiled from man," creates something now-a-days of the astonishment, ridicule, or anger which the denial of a religious dogma does in a society with a fixed religion. Thus, men in England to-day confidently regard the future of the earth for, let us say, the next hundred years in a certain light. Certain countries (especially new countries) are to increase in a regular manner in value and population and property. Certain other countries are to continue their decline. Certain forms of mechanical perfection are to increase, certain speculations as to the nature of the soul are to decline in interest. But more than any particular set of opinions, there is a general colour stamped upon the future in the modern mind, and how securely it is stamped one can best prove by the amusement or surprise that is caused if one suggests (but does not affirm) that there may be (not that there must be) some totally new philosophy, new religion, or new development within three generations.

A book recently published suggests to me the permanent and ironical value of that old tag " The future is veiled from man." It is a study of two somewhat obscure individuals who were members of the Revolutionary Tribunal. It is a very detailed study in which one feels in every page the things that were taken for granted in that place and time —in the Paris of the Revolution. What of all that has come to pass? What of all the fixed certitudes as to the future—nay, the fixed certitudes upon the very nature of man from which, as of necessity, the future was deduced, has remained? The author has done all the better in his study of Vilate and Trinchard from the fact that his position in the Archives has permitted him to look into the ultimate details of the period. But not so much the high historical value of the work as its permanent human lesson strikes me as I read.

Vilate was twenty-four when the great war of the Revolution against the Kings was within a month of breaking out, and when he set out for Paris from the lovely rocky pasturage of his province, up beyond Limoges. And this was what he had in his mind : that the revolutionary movement, to use his own words, "must give to the whole world a spur of insurrection against the oppressors of men." This pathetic certitude was nothing peculiar to the very commonplace young fellow who was leaving his pro-

On the Effect of Time

fessorship in the Indre for Paris. To him they then seemed as much a commonplace as would seem to some young fellow in a similar position to-day in Birmingham some phase about the development of the West of Canada, or some certain prophecy that nations would enrich themselves in proportion to the amount of coal and iron discovered upon their territories.

When Vilate hears a speech in the Revolutionary Parliament he says : " Truth has now appeared and is fixed for ever. It can now call to its tribunal every abuse, every vice, and every crime." Has truth done that in the last hundred years? Yet to Vilate the prophecy of what the Revolution was about to do seemed—and not only to him, but to millions of his contemporaries—as simple as some prophecy of ours about the future of communications ; and he was as easily persuaded that what he said was true as we are that the North temperate climate (and especially that part of Europe which is insular and lies between parallels 50 and 60) is the natural climatic seat of human energy.

Consider again this, which is not from Vilate's own pen, but which occurs in the study before me and is of the first interest : Vilate was in the jury on that day. It was the 9th of February, 1794. Seven Carmelite nuns had refused to take the civic oath to the Republic. The judge made a very commonplace and, as it seemed then, a very sensible speech, pointing out that they were perfectly free to observe the

vows they had taken, that nothing had disappeared
in their lives except the particular convent with which
they were associated; that none of their prejudices
would be offended. And he pointed out that in the
society in which he believed they would have the
sense to live, all men would now be permanently
free. The nuns refused; they refused because the
oath would involve them in schism. How many
men at that time surrounding Vilate had the
slightest conception of what the renascence of
religion was to be in the city of Paris? These
women, members or servants of the little reactionary
aristocratic clique into which the monastic institution
had declined, seemed mere fanatics not only to
Vilate but to the whole of his society. Could you
suddenly have shown Vilate how Europe would still
be raging upon those ultimate questions of religion
more than three generations later; could you have
presented him with the sight of a whole society
divided upon so simple and, as it was then thought,
so irrational a point—what would he have thought?
I can tell you what he would have thought. No
matter what your credentials as a prophet, he would
have thought your prophecy mad. Though you
should have carried him into our very time and given
every proof of the reality of his vision, he would
have woken up to believe it an illusion and a silly
dream.

The state of mind of Trinchard is even more
impressive, because Trinchard was an even smaller,

On the Effect of Time

more commonplace, and therefore more typical, man.
He sat side by side with Vilate in the jury of the
Revolutionary Tribunal. Trinchard was a carpenter.
He was somewhat over thirty years of age at the
period of the Revolution. His brother was a gunner,
fighting against the Vendéans, just at that moment
when Valenciennes had fallen, and when all seemed
over with the Republic; and his brother used to
write from the armies, signing "Your brother, a true
Republican." Two months later he was judging
Marie Antoinette. He wrote to his brother a letter
immediately after the trial. M. Dunoyer publishes
in his book (*Deux Jurés du Tribunal Révolutionnaire*)
a facsimile of that letter, and wonderful reading it
makes. One might put its bad spelling and street
language into modern English something like this:
" I'm learning you, brother, that I was one of them
jurymen as judged the wilbeast what was wolfing a
gurt part of the empire." And so forth. But the
man is doing nothing exceptional. He no more
thinks of himself as exceptional than does any leader-
writer to-day writing upon the virtues or vices of a
contemporary politician in more moderate language.
And note you, as a hundred years can make men
more temperate, so they can make men more violent,
and our modern absence of emphasis may astound
our great-grandchildren quite as much as that revolutionary violence astounds us.

A friend writes to him in that spring of 1794
(when Danton died, and when every man was

51   E 2

occupied in the defence or in the destruction of the Republic). He is a very ordinary friend, his name is Ploton, a Southerner, as Trinchard was. He corresponds more or less in that society to, let us say, a young village shopkeeper in our own, full of a simple patriotism, and especially full of what the Press tells him. And he heads his letter thus: " Second of Germinal, the second year of the Republic—which is as imperishable as the world." What rhetoric ! Nay, to us reading such stuff to-day, what lunacy ! But do not be too sure. Go to the British Museum when you can find an idle afternoon and look up your newspapers of September, 1899, and you will read some amusing phrases.

The truth is that men pass under strong influences of time that fill them more than with wine, rather with an entirety of life. The time in which a man lives may be an exalted time or a weary one, but it fills him altogether, whether it is on fire or drowned. He can conceive, as a rule, nothing in the future different from the temper of his time, though there is all the past to teach him his folly. If he makes a picture of the future, that picture is a mere extension of his own tiny and ephemeral experience, and the more confidently certain he is of that future the more rigidly is it seen by the critical onlooker to be a puppet dressed up in the clothes of the present.

All these things Dunoyer's careful book upon two men of the Revolutionary Tribunal, a monograph characteristic of that ceaseless and immense research

On the Effect of Time

which dignifies the modern French School of History, has suggested to my mind.

Now, whenever I read of the Revolution, in general or in particular, while that lesson of the folly of prophecy perpetually returns to me, yet something else rises from the page. In a certain sense, almost in a mystical sense, the periods of profound faith in a particular future were right. Not because the picture that they saw was true, but because those things outside time upon which they relied were and are true. And even to-day in the sheer anarchy and welter of the time we suffer there is a method of thought which has anchoring ground in the permanent fate of mankind. But what that method may be there is no space to discuss here.

ON A POET

THE days in which Swinburne died, it was remarked by all, were days peculiar to the air and to the landscape which had inspired his verse. One riding in those days upon the high ridges of the New Forest saw before him in the distant hills of Dorset and of Wilts, in the very clear line of the Island, in the belt of sea, and in the great billows of oak woods and of beech that lift up from the hollows, in the clear wind and the new large clouds of spring before it, everything which his poetry meant to those who were of one tongue with him, and all that part of it which, though not incommunicable to foreigners, made him the least translatable of modern writers. Nowhere was it easier to understand what influences had made, or rather driven, his form of expression than on those heights looking towards those hills, and under such a sky, feeling that wind come right from off the English sea.

For it is the chief characteristic of Swinburne's work, and the one which will be noted of him throughout whatever changes the future may bring to our taste, that his motive (if one may use this metaphor) was the landscape and the air of England —especially of South England and of that very roll of land from the chalk to the chalk, from the northern Avon of Wiltshire to the cliffs of the Island which a man surveys from the ridges of which I speak.

Let it not be forgotten that revolutions in taste are among the most certain as they are among the most mysterious proofs of the power of rapid change combined with unity which is peculiar to Europe, and which has been discovered in no other civilisations than that of the Europeans. Only some very few have escaped the chastening of that reflection. There are indeed some classics—one might count them upon the fingers of both hands—which no transition of taste much raises or much diminishes, and chief among these is the sovereignty of Homer. But almost all the others do suffer violent neglects, nay, may be for a generation and more violently despised ; or again, violently adored. And so rapid are these fluctuations of opinion—and so sincere while they remain—that we must always approach with extreme care the criticism of a contemporary. The fluctuations of opinion will at last decide an average. Truth will be plotted out, a clear and intellectual thing, from the welter of mere stimulus. Criticism will acquire, and with every new critic acquire further, certitudes and fixed points of judgment ; and the reputation of a great poet is moulded and informed by the process of time, as all other worthy things are moulded and informed by the process of time. Let us attempt then to stand apart from the feeling of the moment and to ask ourselves what certainly was present in the work of the great writer who died in this uprush of new weather, and this invitation to life that was sweeping over his own land. It is by qualities which, whether we approve them or disapprove, are certainly present in a writer that his reputation with posterity will be made, not by the emotions of the moment which those qualities arouse; nor is any great writer (nor any small one, for that matter) to be judged in general terms, but in particular—since writing is like a man's voice, and always has in it, no matter who produces it, if it be closely examined, characters not general but individual. A man who should have resisted the wave of enthusiasm for Lord Byron, but who should carefully have noted what at any rate he *was*, what his verse was and what it was not, who should have distinguished between what he certainly did easily and what he as certainly could not do, might have praised too much or too little, but that which his analysis had distinguished would enable him to know more or less what kind of posterity would judge Byron, and how. He would have been able to guess, for instance, that a time of youth and of *largesse* would have drunk him in great draughts, a time of age and of exactitude would have found in him a mere looseness of words; he would have been able to see why foreigners especially could discover his greatness;

why the reading of him was proper to a time of active and physical combat against oppression, was improper to any nation which a long peace had corrupted, or to any class which the opportunity for every licence and the power through wealth to approach every enjoyment had satiated and cloyed.

If we so examine Swinburne we shall, as I have said, first notice that in all his work the mere nature of South England drives him. It is the expression often uncontrolled, always spontaneous, of an intense communion with that air, those colours, such hills and such a sea. In this Swinburne, wholly novel as was his medium of expression, was peculiarly and rigidly national. Whoever best knows that landscape and that sky best feels him. Whoever in the future most neglects it or knows it least will least fully appreciate or will perhaps even neglect his work. In whatever times the inspiration of that belt of land weakens in the men who inhabit it (it weakened in the Eighteenth Century, for instance), in such a time the influence of Swinburne's work will weaken too.

Next there must be noted that in him much more than in any other writer of the language, or, at any rate, much more than in any other modern writer of prominence, words followed rhythm, and the poem, though an organised and constructed thing, went bowling before the general music of its metre as a ship over-canvased goes bowling before the general gale. That music underlies all lyrical expression,

and for that matter poetry of every other kind as
well, all critics have always known. But it is
modern to make of it, as it were, the necessary and
conscious substructure of the work, and Verlaine,
who put it in his Poetic Art as the chief rule to consider " Music and always Music," was, in laying down
such a law, the extreme expression of his time.
Sense is not sacrificed wholly in any place, it is
but rarely imperilled even by this motive in
Swinburne. But one feels that reason has in the
construction no divine place, but is subsidiary—as
it is subsidiary in unworded tunes, as it is subsidiary
in great and vivid dreams, as it is subsidiary (since
one should be just even in judging extravagance) in
all the major emotions of the human soul : in love,
in combat, in despair. And in this necessary service
of rhythm, this bondage to music, is to be discovered
the source of another characteristic in the work : the
perpetual repetition. Two men, both sedulous and
scholarly admirers, will be equally struck by the
apparently contradictory judgments that Swinburne
was unequalled in the range of his vocabulary, and
that Swinburne was, quite beyond parallel, repeti-
tive. Each judgment would strike one of the two
types of admirer as a paradox or a truism. Yet both
are true, and both have an illuminating meaning
when his work is considered. That vast vocabulary
(and if you will be at the pains to note word upon
word or to make a short concordance you will see that
the word " vast " is just)—that vast vocabulary, I say,

proceeded from the necessity of satisfying the ear. An exact shade of length and emphasis were needed ; they must be exactly filled, and some one word out of the thousands upon thousands which the numerically richest language of our time possesses must be hit upon to do the work. This surely was the source of that wide range. So also was it the source of the repetition.

Repetition is discovered in literature under two aspects. It is deliberate and admiringly designed, or it is involuntary and an odious symptom of fatigue. The repetitions of Catullus in their way, the repetitions of the Hebrew poets in theirs, were meant to be ; or rather (for their voluntary quality is obvious) they were exactly designed to produce a particular effect, and did produce it ; the repetition of those who fail, involuntary and symptomatic of fatigue, may be neglected. Swinburne's repetitions were neither of the one kind nor of the other ; they were the recurrence of a set of words or of single words which suited the sound in his head. And just as to fit exactly a void of known form one word exactly fitting must be found (fitting not reason but the ear) so those which had been found to fit particular rhythms must be used again to fit those rhythms when they recurred, as naturally and as necessarily as a man picks up this tool and that to do some particular bit of carving which he has found it apt for in the past. The word in Swinburne was subordinate.

It is a commonplace, and a true one—to pass to

another matter—that the English writers of the later Nineteenth Century (and not the writers alone) reposed upon the Jacobean translation of the Old Testament. That unique and fundamental piece of work, the monumental characters in which appear more largely with every process of retreat from it, whether in time or in conviction, has so formed that generation that it was itself almost unconscious of the enormous effect. Swinburne is as full of it as Kipling; the ready-made phrases of weary political discussion are full of it. The whole national life, in so far as modes of expression are concerned, was filled with it. Many of Swinburne's rhythms were the rhythms of the English Psaltry, and perpetually you will find some sounding final phrase, especially if it ends in an interrogation, to be a phrase of biblical character or even a biblical transcription. Herein, again, as in that effect of landscape and of air, he is national in every particle of his poetic being; and one may remark that this note is the note of unity in him, and that a recognition of it explains what has confused so many critics of his life and of his opinion. The man who in youth was ardent for a liberty which leant much nearer to anarchy than to the republic, who ranged, as the fashion was over all Europe, to find subjects for that mood, in age perpetually sounded a note which had in it something exaggerated of fury and of protest against whatever might be thought to be weakening the very old and fixed boundaries of the national

life. Yet it was the same man whose extreme
facility poured out in either field ; the passionate
protest of the first years was a protest drawn from
the untrammelled nature about him which ran
through him and made him write. The convinced
and extreme political insistence of his later verse
was drawn from the same source. It was still the
surroundings of his own land that compelled him.

There is one last thing to be said : the work has
been called pagan. It is the commonest praise or
blame attached to the achievement. Those who
attach it, whether in praise or blame, have not clearly
seen the pagan world. By pagan we mean that
long, long manhood of Europe (a thousand years
long to our knowledge—how much longer we know
not) in which the mind certainly reposed and was
certainly in tune with the nature of the Mediterranean. Swinburne's great love of that mood was
the love of a foreigner, of a much belated man, and
of a man of the North. The sea of the Atalanta in
Calydon is an English sea. All that attitude in him
was reaction and a protest. It was full of yearning :
now pagan paganism was not full of this. The very
earliest moment in which a protest of that kind is
to be found is the Fourth Century. For the transformation between the old and the new lay in this,
that there came upon our race in the first four centuries of the Roman Empire a yearning which must
be satisfied, and men since then have accepted an
assuagement of it or have passionately protested

against that assuagement, or have cynically ridiculed it, but they have never remained other than
profoundly influenced by it. What is called
" paganism " since that change came is not of
marble and is not calm : it is a product, not of the
old time, but of the new.

ON A PROPHET

YEARS ago in the county of Kent a gentleman of
means, culture and lineage begged me to make the
acquaintance of a certain neighbour of his who dwelt
in a little cottage called (by the wrath of God) " The
Hollies "—and, indeed, a holly-tree of no small size,
but one only, grew beside his door. This cottage
was cubical in formation with the exception of the
roof, which was a pyramid, and it was built of brick
with the exception of the roof, which was of slate.
Its name, " The Hollies," was painted outside upon
the gate. This is all I have to say about the
cottage.

The man who dwelt within it came that very
evening to dine at the Squire's, and was what you
will call obviously a gentleman. He was not a
gentleman in any cryptic or mystical sense; he was
not the Adumbration of a gentleman; he was not the
Platonic Idea of a gentleman; he was not the
Gentleman used loosely as a term for a good man;
he was not rich; he spoke perfectly; he was very
stupid. Much more than this, he was a Prophet.

The learned have observed (or at least the only

ones among them who count have persistently
observed) that it is in the nature of barbaric peoples
to accept whatever is told them with sufficient
assurance, conviction and simplicity, but especially
if it regard the future. On this account (the learned
say) he who will prophesy with flame shall certainly
among barbarians become a founder. Now it is
sufficiently certain that this type of man, so successful among the primitive, and perhaps also among
the decayed, continues through all ages and in all
societies, though varying perhaps in proportion, and
certainly varying enormously in the source of his
information according to the generation in which he
lives, is here to-day ; and this man was one of him.

At first I did not know in what a Presence I stood
—or rather sat—for he was very modest, if indeed it
be modest to make no noise in the eating of soup, to
frown heavily, and never to speak a word. There
were but three of us there, the Squire, myself, *et
Rex Meus* the Prophet. Having seen little of the
world I much desired to hear what he would say ;
although he was still what politicians call young he
seemed old to me, because he had a full beard, and
because life had already wearied him, a thing incom-
prehensible to boys. The Squire watched him with
a good deal of admiration and of fear, until at last
he said, "There won't be any war." Here let me
tell you that these words were pronounced in the
year 1888, and a little before the bursting of the
spring upon the Kentish Weald.

On a Prophet

Nor was there one. There was no war about that time.

Those who read these lines, I am quite certain, will find them a shock. We live in a time when war is so struck with doom that it is putting on speed, as it were, to make a fine ending. War is out of our manners; we can tolerate it no more. Every year is a new reconciliation, and a new treaty in the federation of all mankind except those who have neglected their armament, and in general we are forgetting war. But there have been wars, and of some calibre—hefty and noisy wars since you and I were boys. Now in 1888 there was no war. So the Prophet was right.

The Squire was interested and humble, and being a plain man he asked why there would be no war, for it was imagined at that moment by eight or nine newspaper men that some war or other was going to break out; but what war I forget after such a lapse of time. The Prophet was a true prophet, by which I do not mean that he prophesied truth, but only that he was in keeping with all that I have ever read of his breed; he shook his doormat of a head and wagged his beard, smiling, as bearded men do, with the eyes only, and would give no reasons; and, indeed, there was no war. But as the dinner went on he talked of other things; he prophesied a Parliament in Dublin " within ten years," and, new as I was to the world, I could but note how much of his conversation worked within fixed frames and limits,

On Anything

as should beseem a prophet. Some things were
going to happen "within five years," some "within
twenty years," some—and the leap was indeed
splendid—"within fifty years." Among these last
I dimly remember was the spread of a universal
language, which I think he called "Anglo-Saxon";
and there was something or other about the birth-
rate which escapes me now, but which I can
remember to have appalled me at the time, for it
was a destruction of all I loved and revered in
Europe.

The dinner went on, and as he got more food and
wine into him he prophesied less—for fasting is the
mother of prophecy. He was still assertive, he was
still sure; his talk was still of public men, of con-
tinents, of armies, of battle and of sudden death,
but the future entered less into it, and the present
more. He became not so much a prophet, but, if I
may use the word quite gently, more of a liar. I can
remember vividly now, after so many years, how he
stood in the hall of that great house, all wrapped up
to go through the park to "The Hollies." I looked
at his large frame and masterful demeanour. I
remembered all that he had said, both of things
distant from me and of things to come, and I
admired such eyes in the brain.

It was ten years before I met him again. I am
wrong—it was nine. I met him upon a steamboat
in the North Sea, and he remembered me. We
looked over the side of the ship and talked about

On a Prophet

America and Spain. As to the chance of war he waved it all away with his hand. It might come or it might not [the truth was, it was too near for his type of vision], but what would come *after*, whether the war was fought or not, was quite clear. " America," he said, " would learn that she could fight a European Power." It seems that having learnt this, all sorts of things would happen, and there would be banging and bingeing to some tune. The earning of one's living, the weight and dullness which come upon the mind from seeing too many places and knowing too many men, left my impression less vivid. For, as it says in the song—

> Ki moulte y resve mainte a vu :
> Ki pleure trop a trop vescu.

But anyhow there remains to me the impression of that conflict between the Old World and the New which I was destined to experience, and which I in no way desired. He had been following French politics also, and he told me—not by way of prophecy, but as a revelation of inner truth—why it was that Germany had not declared war upon France and taken Paris in the autumn of the preceding year. I talked to him, therefore, of the 75mm. gun. He did not shirk it. He talked of it as one who knew : and as I heard him my mind grew aged. I left him in a port of Holland after luncheon, and the last I remember of him on that occasion was a slight gesture of his from the wrist only (for he was a

dignified man) explaining how all that I saw, the
port, the shipping, the docks, everything, would be
German " within ten years."

I met him again several times in the succeeding
waves of our century. I met him just before the
Boer War, and a little after Colenso. He prophesied
only upon one matter upon these occasions, and
that was the length of the conflict, which, with an
exact discrimination, he invariably placed within
" six months " of the day upon which he addressed
me, and the third time he assured me of this thing
was in the month of February 1902, and that time
he was right.

Since then I have met him continually, for he
knows less people than he used to do, and he has
fallen into a routine of old friends. The Squire is
dead, and he only goes down to " The Hollies " now
and again. It is his pleasure still to foresee. The
war over, he bought Consols. He was careful to
explain that he was no fool. They were at 97.
They would fall, of course ; he was not buying for
immediate rise. In part of this anticipation he was
not disappointed, but in another part he was. He
was in a fume for some little time about an approaching war with Russia upon the frontiers of India, and
again he would return to that recurrent theme of his
life, the destruction of all limitrophous civilisations
by the organised might of Germany. But his chief
concern was the march of China upon Europe, which,
as he clearly foresaw, could not be long delayed.

On a Prophet

" That," he said, with a sort of Christian enthusiasm,
" would bind us all together once more ! "

Whether it be a labour to prophesy or no, his
hair had certainly grown white in the pursuit of
his vocation, and when I last saw him (which was
a little after the Epiphany in Rugby Station, waiting
for the train to Carlisle) we spent ten minutes together, and he told me with unabated gladness that
war would break out in the Balkans " when the snow
melted." I asked him at what time this change
came about in the Balkans, but he did not know.

ON BELIEVING

WHENEVER one studies, even superficially, any generation of men who have acted in the past and of whose actions there is some considerable record, that, I think, which most strikes the curious student is the nature of the things which were taken for granted during the period.

Very much might be written—whole books—upon the effects which this has upon history. Innumerable points arise as one considers it. For instance, there is no case I can remember of the things which were taken for granted existing in the same plenitude of record as the other things of history. The men of the Ninth Century did not sit down formally and tell us that they looked at the world in such and such a fashion. We have to glean and to pick out their standpoint by working parallel, noting unconscious expressions and side effects. It is like watching a man speaking on some matter of minor interest and trying to define through his tone and gesture the standpoint from which not only that minor interest, but every other, is regarded by his mind.

On Believing

Perhaps nothing is more subject to close scrutiny to-day, is more suspected, and has more difficulty in establishing itself than an unusual physical experience, especially if there be about it a suspicion of connection with the nature and destiny of the human soul. There are certain periods in human history—the end of the Roman Empire is one of them; the beginning, or at least the very early dawn, of the Middle Ages was another—when marvels of this kind were sought after and met, as it were, half way by the mind of the time. The marvellous ran through the spirit of those generations very much as the accumulation of the ascertained, common and often unimportant, fact runs through the spirit of our time. They accumulated legend and what must, in the vast majority of cases, have been even falsehood with the same readiness with which we accumulate columns of statistics. They believed certain types of things to be true, and that belief led them to accept very much of the same nature on which they had no proof.

A very excellent example of the changes which take place from one generation to another in this respect may be discovered by any one who will set himself out to answer this question: "What did Englishmen in the middle and end of the Twelfth Century think about property in land?" Note the conditions of the problem. Land was the all-important thing of the time. It was the one thing on which men left records which they were deter-

mined should be minute, accurate and permanent.
Yet there is no scholar at once so learned and so
wise that he can with any exactitude answer the
question. And it is evident that the fascination of
the subject chiefly lies in the limitless field which it
opens for discussion. There are those—excellent
scholars—who will have it that the Englishmen of
that time thought of land fundamentally as something common to the community. There are others
—scholars of perhaps equal standing—who will have
it that the Roman conception of absolute ownership
had survived in nearly all its original simplicity.
Between these two extremes scholarship may range
at will; and however certain one may be individually
that one's own point of view is right, one will never
be able to marshal proof which shall certainly convince, and finally convince, the whole of the learned
world. The men of that time believed something
about land. They never set it down, they took it
for granted; and we can only judge of what that
belief was by its secondary effects. It sounds
amazing, but it is true.

Another character of this unseizable spirit of the
time is the distortion it appears to produce in morals
when one is looking at it through the medium of
another spirit belonging to another time—our own.

No one can read the history of the French
Revolution without perceiving that certain doctrines
of comparatively little effect upon the material circumstance of men so entirely filled the whole mental

On Believing

atmosphere of the great bulk of the French people, and certainly of a very large proportion of Western Europe in general, as to mould the whole of thought. We can name those doctrines, we can talk of "equality"—a dogma which may be true or false, but is certainly transcendental ; we may talk as they talked about "liberty," but that does not give us any conception of the colour, smell, atmosphere, of the thing that drove them. And unless the reader is in touch with that evasive and central thing in the period it becomes an inexplicable welter : the inexplicable welter which so many of our school and university text-books make of it. A man (apparently a poor orator) moves men to frenzy—Robespierre. Another, a somewhat over-refined scientist of good birth and excellent balance of mind, is the first to propose the total dissolution of all the most ancient organs of the State and the destruction of the Monarchy. A third, an honest little lawyer, anxious to keep his little family, appears like a tiger ravening for blood. A fourth, a linendraper in Limoges, is put at the head of an army of 85,000 men and wins one victory after another. It is an amazing dance of impossible results following upon incredible causes —unless one has the spirit ; and if one has it, as Michelet had it, the whole thing can be presented, not only in proportion and in orders, but actually with splendour.

You have something of the same kind in the contemplation of what are to us the atrocious cruelties of the Fifteenth Century. You do not find those cruelties striking the imagination of the time. You find injustice denounced, approaching chastisement prophesied, all the symptoms of a diseased society in the rulers and great vitality that perceived that disease among the oppressed, but what you do *not* get specifically mentioned, or at any rate not mentioned with reiteration, is the cruelty which to us as we read of it seems something quite remote from human habit or experience. Men and women are burnt alive in numbers which steadily increase from that time to the first generation of the Seventeenth Century. They are not thus tortured by the ferocity of the mob. The thing is done quite quietly by process of law, exactly as one might distrain for debt. You will perpetually hear vigorous protests against the justice of some particular sentence, but you will very rarely (but for the fear of such a negative, I should say never) find men saying "just or unjust, the cruelty of the execution is so revolting that I protest against it." Men believed something with regard to the whole doctrine of expiation, of penal arrangements which they have not described to us and which we cannot understand save through glimpses, side-lights, and careful deductions from or guesses through what they imagine to be their plainest statements. Thus in the particular case of burning alive—a thing we can scarcely bear to contemplate even in words—the framers of the statutes seem to have thought not of

the thing as a horror but as a particular type of
execution symbolic of the total destruction of the
culprit.   It is quite easy to prove, from numerous
instances—Savonarola is one in point—that the
judges often appeared indifferent whether the body
consumed were alive or dead. The chance pity of
spectators in some cases, the sentence of the court
in others, is permitted to release the sufferer long
before the flames. To us it is amazing that such an
attitude towards such a pain could have existed, but
it did exist.

Now the moral of such suggestions (and they crop
up innumerable all over the surface of historical
study) is that our own time lives in such an atmosphere and cannot define it. One would imagine in
the torrent of printing and of record that everything
concerning our time would be fixed and known.
The most fundamental thing of all will not be fixed
and known : it will have to be imperfectly guessed
at. Some chance student in some particular era of
posterity will say : " These people were more concerned with questions of property, apparently, than
with religion. That is madness—but let us see
what kind of madness it was and work out its nature,
since they never clearly set down how they got into
such a frame of mind nor even what that frame of
mind was." Or another student will say in another
epoch : " These people hesitated before personal
combat—the most rational and commonplace of
daily happenings. It is amazing, but it is true

On Anything

Let me ferret out the state of mind which can have produced such an abnormal result." And so forth. Our time, like all those past times, will be watched curiously, and this mysterious thing will be sought and hardly found. The irony lies in this: that the spirit posterity will so seek is in us, here, to-day— and we cannot express it.

ON THE AIR OF THE
DORDOGNE

ALL countries are built in vast inclined planes which lean up against one another and have ridges between. The great rivers run in the hollows where these planes meet at their lowest, and the watersheds are the lines along which their top edges come together—and there, you might think, was the end of it : but there is much more.

You must not only say : " I have left the valley of the Thames, I have found the valley of the Itchen," nor only : " I have come over St. Leonards Forest ; I am no longer among the Surrey rivers, I am on the headwaters of the Sussex Weald," nor only : " I have left the great fields of the Yonne and the Seine and I have come down on to the Plain of Burgundy and the Eastern Rivers "—it is much more than that.

The slope that looks northward is one thing, the slope that looks southward another. The slope that has been conquered or ordered by the foreigner, or civilised from without, or in any way rearranged, may march with, but will contrast violently against,

77

the slope that has been protected or isolated or left desert.

The very storms of Nature treat one and the other differently; the rivers do a different work according to the treatment of forests by men within their watershed; the soil sometimes, the air always, changes. Above all, the houses of men change.

The accent of speech changes, if not the form of speech; nay, in the transition from one such region to another I can believe that the daylight seems to change.

All those subtle, permanent, and masterly things which we cannot measure, but which are infinitely important compared with what we can measure, are grouped in groups in those great depressions which look to one sea or to one city, and the regions of Europe and its patriotisms run ultimately with the valleys. So it is with the Loire, and the Dordogne.

Whatever feeds the Loire is one. There are large uncultivated heaths the size of a country; there are very quiet pastures, very rich and silent, stretching for a hundred miles and as broad as a man would care to walk in a day; and in the highlands of the watershed there are rocks, and the trees of rocks, and at last sterile and savage mountains. And the upper courses of all the rivers of the Loire are torrents foaming in glens. Nevertheless, whatever feeds the Loire has a unity. The Allier, the Vienne, the Creuse, the Loire itself (which is only one stream out of many) are bound together.

On the Air of the Dordogne

Well, you go up into the sources of the watershed, you cross a confused land of rounded hills and knobs of crested rock and short, sturdy, sparse wood and heather and broom, and at last you see at your feet, trickling southward, not northwards, a stream that knows its way. And this at last, when it has worked its way through little waterfalls and past the gates it knows, will be the River Isle. If you knew it only from the map you would think it a stream like any other stream, but when you go downwards with it upon your feet, and when you see it with your eyes, tumbling and hurrying there, you know that everything has changed—you are in the air of the Dordogne.

There is a louder noise in the village streets ; the habit of summer clings to them late into the winter time and re-arises in them early with the spring—though the cold is sharp in all the hills of the Limousin, whether to the north or to the south of that watershed, yet the south of it has a tradition very different from the north, and the sun is more kind or more worshipped. Here are lodges built beside or over the humblest houses ; the vine is not so disciplined ; it has a simpler and a more natural growth, it is an ornament and a shade. The churches have flat roofs such as Italy and Spain will use. Their Gothic is an attempt, their Romanesque is native.

The children and the birds are careless. Wealth is not spent in luxury but in externals, and proverty is contented. All this is the air of the Dordogne.

On Anything

You feel what you have come to when you drink your first cup of wine on the southward slope of the hill, for the wine of every country is the soul of it. No Romans caught these men to plant the vine, it was surely native here. Here the vine grudges nothing; the god who inhabits it is not here a guest or a prisoner. Its juice is full and admirable. It needs no age. In Burgundy, where an iron works in the earth, they need nine years to breed perfection in their wine, but here, in the air of the Dordogne, though so far south, they need not seven. Within twelve months of the vintage a stranger can hardly tell its age, and for my part I would drink it gladly in November with the people there.

God forbid that any one should blaspheme the wines of the Loire, the cherished and difficult vineyards of Touraine. Great care and many friends protect them, and an infinite labour brings them to maturity. The wine of Chinon, which made Rabelais, the wine of Vouvray, which is good for the studying of mathematics, the wine of Saumur, which teaches men how to leap horses over gates—all these wines are of the north, and yet it would be treason to malign them.

I will not be tempted to such a treason, but could I be tempted I should be tempted by the generous invitation which, when one comes down the southward slope and feels the air of the Dordogne, proceeds and gathers from the vineyards of that delightful land. You may have seen on bottles the

On the Air of the Dordogne

word "St. Emilion," and if what was within was from St. Emilion indeed, then you saw a great name upon the label; for you must know that St. Emilion is built in a sacred hollow. There Guadet, "who could not forgive," was born. Thence the noblest blood of the Revolution proceeded. In its vineyards died by their own hand the best of the Republicans, and this place still keeps, as in a kind of chalice, the spirit of the Gironde. If you doubt it, drink the wine. And St. Emilion is, as it were, the centre and navel of the country of the Dordogne. Here there stands or stood a church built all out of one rock. St. Martin, or some such person, beginning the monastic habit, was pestered (I have heard) by the grand nobles whom he had persuaded to monkishness in a fit of piety, for they said: "This life of yours is all very well, but what is there to do?"

Then St. Martin, lifting up his eyes, saw a large rock, and said to the youngest of them—

"Here is a great rock. Hack it about and chisel it until it has the shape of a church outside, and then cut doors and windows and hack away into it until it has the shape of a church inside, and you will have plenty to do."

The story as it was told to me goes on to say that they lived to be so old and so very old at their labour that they saw Charlemagne go riding by before the first Mass was sung in that rock church; and that that great soldier, coming in to their first

On Anything

Mass, thought the workers in their extreme old age to be the spirits of another world.

Now the church of St. Emilion is a symbol of the air of the Dordogne on account of its strength, its homogeneity, its legend, and its virtue of delicate but profound age.

You have drunk Barsac—and in so drinking you drank (you thought) April woods and the first flowers. Barsac would not be Barsac but for the Dordogne, which helps to make the great Gironde. And you have drunk Entremer, which is the name for a host of wines, but the kernel of the whole thing is the full blood that dreams and ripens, and as it were procreates, where the slope of the Dordogne is most the Dordogne, although the Dordogne is not there : at St. Emilion.

The pen has the power to describe, not general, but particular things. Though it may define what is general, it can call up only what is particular, and in that extended province which is ruled by the Dordogne St. Emilion has moved me to a particular description.

ON THE SITES OF THE REVOLUTION

THERE is not in travel an interest more fascinating than that of noting with the eyes and proving by the memory and by books the exact place of great or decisive actions. So have I just done in many places. Here (I have said to myself) Abdul-ul-Rahman went up Aragon till he came to the head of the Pass. Here he first saw the plains of Gaul from a height and promised himself the conquest of all Europe for Islam. Here, where the two rivers meet somewhat north of Poitiers, the two hosts watched each other for a week, and that which was not ours was defeated.

Then again, in Toulouse it was amazing to collect, as one wandered through, the memories of so many centuries. Here were the shrine where the body of Saturninus was found dead, dragged to death by a bull through the streets of the city ; the quarter from which the populace saw advancing the Northern Army that was to defeat the Visigoths; the site of the wall whence the retreat of the Saracen was noted, a flood of men pouring back towards the wall of the

On Anything

Pyrenees; the flat heights beyond the city to the east, where the English Army came up from Spain in the defeats of Napoleon and drove back the resistance of the defence.

All these, and many more, a man notes in a travel of but few days, for all Europe—and no province more than this—is crammed with the story of its own past; but perhaps that which, in such reminiscences or resurrections, most moves one is to observe the obliteration of the last and most immediate of our efforts. The sites of the Revolution have disappeared.

One may walk about Paris—as I have walked to-day—and see stones and windows that are still alive with the long business of the city. There is the room where Madame de Sévigné wrote, there is the long gallery where Sully paced, recognising the new power of artillery and planning the greatness of his master. You may stand on the very floor where the priests stood when St. Louis held the Crown of Thorns above them, more than six hundred years ago; you may stand on the stone that covers Geoffrey Plantagenet before the altar of the Cathedral; you may touch the altar that the boatmen raised under Tiberius to their gods when our Lord was preaching in Galilee, and as you marvel at that stone you may note around you the little Roman bricks that stood in the same arches when Julian saw them, sitting at the Council that saved the Faith for the West.

All these old things remain in this moving, and yet

On the Sites of the Revolution

unchanging, town—except the things of its principal and most memorable feat of will.

The Revolution is even now not old. Its effects are still in movement; they are not yet accomplished. Of the fundamental quarrels which it raised (some five or six) one at least, that of religion, is by no means resolved.

• It is not even old in time. I who write this have known some who saw it; many who remembered its soldiers or its victims. I have but to-day visited a room where a daughter of the Montgolfiers would tell me in her extreme old age how the mob poured on the Bastille, and her companion, nearer to me in blood, had seen, and in my boyhood talked to me of, Napoleon. How many all round me, to-day or yesterday, were filled with the light or fire of that time, saying, " My father died in such and such a battle," in Spain, or in Italy, or beyond the Vistula —at the ends of the world. It is not so very long ago. It was much the chief business, for good or evil, that Europe has known since the Empire accepted the Faith. And what visible relics of it remain ?

Where the National Assembly sat at Versailles, the Salle des Menus Plaisirs, there are a few houses or barracks, a place in building. Where they sat in Paris, they and the first days of the Convention, wrestling with and throwing Necessity, the Riding School, that vast oval cavern in which they forged the modern world, has utterly gone.

On Anything

I never pass the place, even hurriedly and on business to some work or other, but I pause a moment to consider so great a change ! It is where the Rue Castiglione comes now into the Rue de Rivoli—two streets whose very names are those of battles fought long after the atlantean work was done. Not a trace remains. A drinking shop for foreign jockeys, a cosmopolitan hotel, a milliner's where the rich of all nations (the women of the rich, that is) go in and buy ; these hold the place. Here Mirabeau spoke his last words with effort and went home to die ; here Verginaud thundered ; here Louis and Mary Antoinette took refuge in the oven of the August days ; here the long vote, a day and a night and yet another day, dragged on and ended with the end of the Capétians—after a thousand years.

The Tuileries saw more. They saw the outlawing of Thermidor, the quarrels that ended in the dictatorship, the hard scuffle that killed the monarchy. They have wholly disappeared. At the one end of them still stands the room where the committee made war on the whole world, and imposed upon the nation that leaden law of armies which we still call the Terror. But for that room all has gone.

The town-hall has gone. It was the focus of the revolt, it led the fever of the war against the kings. From it came the massacres of September — by order, I believe,—into it retreated and was defeated the last effort of extreme equality. This building at

On the Sites of the Revolution

least (one might have hoped) might have been spared
for history. It had sprung from the Renaissance, whole
and beautiful. It had seen all the growths of the
Bourbons and of their power, all the growing con-
sciousness of Paris. It held half the documents of
the city and more than half its destiny. It was
the head, and its Italian front was the face, of Paris.
It has gone altogether. It was burned when the
Tuileries was burned.

The room where Danton pleaded so that his voice
was heard beyond the river; the room where the
Queen, in a voice low and firm, replied to the questions of her judges; the room where Marat was
acquitted, and where the Girondins sang—all that
has gone in fire. The house where Desmoulins first
conspired is pulled down. The house where Danton
sat in his last hours watching the fire and caring
little for life or death has also gone. The Jacobins
are a market-place. The temple was pulled down
by the order of Napoleon. That furious business
seems to have burnt out the very stones of its
origin or to have burst the confines wherein it was
conceived.

Perhaps a fate rested upon them all.

I went to-day through woods that were quite
lonely twenty years ago. They stood near my
home. Here, in the midst of the trees, and in a
deserted place reached by a dismantled and
neglected road, rose a country-house, regular in
outline, monotonous, and faded. The windows were

open to the night, the floors rotten ; green moss grew on the plaster of the walls ; the roof was ruinous. It was the house to which the daughter of Marie Antoinette had come, reserved, and perhaps with terrors in her mind, to find silence while the restoration still endured. It was her refuge. Years after it stood as I have recalled it. I saw it (I say) again to-day—or rather, I saw it no longer.

The woods are felled in regular great roads. There are villas built and new inns, and pleasure-places. A new Paris has spread out towards it and killed it. Here also the memory of the Revolution, the physical memory, has disappeared.

I know of no wave like it in Europe or in the history of Europe : of no such attempt, so great, so full of men and of creation, whose outward garment in building has been so thrust away by the irony of Time.

A SECRET LETTER

I HAD promised Your Excellency in my last dispatch to let him know with the least delay both the consequences of my appeal to the King in this country and the events that might flow from his attitude.

It is with profound sorrow that I communicate to Your Excellency the whole of this passage.

Upon Wednesday, St. James's Day, I was granted an audience by His Majesty at seven in the morning, which is his usual hour for receiving foreign envoys and all those accredited with public or secret powers from another Court.

His Majesty, whom I had not met before, is a man tall in stature, but stooping somewhat at the shoulders. His age is not apparent in his features, his hair and beard (which is scanty) are still black, and his eyes, though they betray an expression of weariness, are lively. He was good enough to bid certain officials near him to go out into the anteroom, where I trust my words could not be heard, though there is no door separating the King's closet from that passage, but only a German tapestry, presented, I think, at the time of the King's marriage by the Elector, his father-in-law.

The King would first have me set before him what I had to say, which I did as briefly as possible, and following exactly the instructions given me by Your Excellency. I made no attempt to diminish, still less to deny the crime of which My Lord had been guilty ; nay, I even exaggerated it, if that were possible, in order to prepare his Sovereign for my plea, which was that My Lord's youth and the manner in which the adventure was presented to him excused him in some part for the action of which he had been guilty. I briefly spoke of the campaigns in which he had fought since his sixteenth year, and I showed how easily to a soldier the expedition which has had so disastrous an ending might have appeared as a just and loyal war. I was careful to omit any whisper of what the Emperor had threatened in case of a refusal (for such were your instructions), and finally I laid at the feet of His Majesty the plea of common mercy, dwelling upon My Lord's household, the future of his young and innocent children, and all else that would follow upon the sacrifice of such a life.

His Majesty listened to me gravely, and replied that he had fully revolved My Lord's action, and its nature and consequence, in his mind, as also the effect of the determination he himself had taken, which determination could not be shaken by any argument that I or another might put before him.

A Secret Letter

It was (he said) a necessary example to others, and the more highly placed the culprit the stronger the necessity of the sentence appeared to him. He said further, that in the matter of rebellion and treason (which, as Holy Writ discovered, was among the most detestable of crimes, and compared even to witchcraft, against which enormity His Majesty is especially watchful) it was a thing which must be ended once and for all, and could not be dealt with in any manner save by the extirpation of its authors and the total suppression and extinction of the originators and begettors thereof. To be brief, His Majesty would not be moved in any manner, but told me, speaking as a man will who has no more to say, the date and hour were already fixed, and had been communicated to me. With this His Majesty dismissed me, and I left him.

Upon the Thursday, therefore, the morrow, which they reckon in this country as the 15th of the month, I bade Charles, my attendant, go warn My Lord that I would see him at his convenience, and My Lord answered very graciously that my convenience was his own, whereupon I said I would come at once, and did so, it being about an hour after noon, and My Lord sitting at wine after his meal, which he had eaten alone in the room assigned to him.

My Lord was well furnished in all particulars, and the clemency of the season further lessened his discomforts of prison, but he was closely guarded, and he complained to me, though without bitterness,

that when his wife had visited him but a week
before, bringing with her the little Count, my
master, and his little sister also by the hand, a man-
at-arms had been present throughout their interview. He also told me that for writing he might
have what liberty he would, but that he might fold
over and seal no letter.   I asked him what his regi-
men had been in the matter of religion, at which he
sighed and said that he had been permitted to see
the Carthusian whom Your Excellency had sent to
this part under a safeguard, but that no Mass might
be said in his room, nor within the precincts of the
whole castle : which, as he was told, was forbidden
by a law of this realm ; but this I would hardly
believe, and indeed we had permission of His
Majesty (who is indifferent to such things) that Mass
should be privily said upon the following morning,
which was that on which My Lord was to suffer.
And for this purpose a table was set, he whom Your
Excellency has sent bringing with him a little altar
stone and all that was necessary for the Office.

My Lord dismissed me when I had spoken to him
for perhaps half-an-hour, asking him what I should
do, but he bade me return a little before sunrise on
the morrow, which (Your Excellency) I very punc-
tually did, more sorrowful at heart than I could say,
having not slept that night for the multitude of
letters that I must read and dispatch, and for the
weight of the business that was before me.

When therefore it was fully light, but the sun not

A Secret Letter

yet risen, I went over from my lodgings (which are
not far from the Royal Mint) to the Castle, and was
admitted to My Lord's presence, where he sat with
a heavy look, and yet gallantly as it were, having
with him My Lady and the two little children, the
Priest having said Mass and the table being now in
order, but he remaining for the last Offices.

My Lady was troubled exceedingly, and a woman
of hers who was with her was but little help to her
or to us. As for My Lord's children, though they
could not understand the case, they saw that something great and terrible was at hand. But all this
should not be detailed to Your Excellency, nor can
my pen properly express it. My Lady and her
servant and the two children were taken, I think,
from the room, but I did not look, nor did I hear
any sound except a slight sobbing, which very soon
ceased : the passing of men-at-arms set at regular
places without I remember to hear continuing, and
if it be a trivial matter to have this set down for
Your Excellency, I do so only in the desire to relate
every particular and to omit nothing. I asked My
Lord whether there was anything that I could further
communicate to the King or to his family, or to
any one. He answered in a firm voice that he had
attended to all. And he gave me a letter sealed
(for this was now permitted him), which letter I am
to deliver to Your Excellency and will do so, since I
must entrust it to no one. He told me further that
he had made his peace and that he had received

On Anything

Communion, but that he would beg the priest whom Your Excellency had sent to remain with him to the end. The Warden of the Castle, a man of strict purpose, but not harsh in his demeanour (though silent, as are the most of these people), said here that the populace, who had gathered in a great crowd, might be angered at the sight of a priest, which sight indeed would recall in them all the circumstances of the war. To this My Lord answered, a little disdainfully I thought, that it was but little to ask, and that for the anger of the people, and indeed for any feeling they might have towards himself, he had no care of it. He did not desire to arouse it, nor did he fear it. Then said the Warden of the Castle, he might be accompanied as he wished, but the priest must put off his gown: which he did and stood dressed like any common man of this country, or rather like some servant. But his hair and the trim of his beard seemed the more foreign in such a habit.

The sun had now risen, and we were apprised that My Lord's hour had come by the beating of drums outside the castle and the noise of the people. My Lord hearing this looked at me sorrowfully for a little time and asked me a question in the matter of religion which I thought both terrible and confusing at such a time, but he pressed me and I replied very humbly that for my part I had lived as most men lived in these times, which are corrupt and evil, and that indeed no man could fully understand the unseen things; no, nor so much as conceive them; but that none the less I hoped I might always bear witness to the Faith as did he at that very moment. To which My Lord answered, sighing, "I bear no witness to that, but only to my constancy, and I could wish that they had left me my sword."

I set down for Your Excellency all that happened, but I would not have Your Excellency think that My Lord was troubled in these matters; only it was his custom to debate learning and philosophy and to express doubts that he might hear them answered: this was all. And it is truly said that a man's custom will be seen expressed in the end of his life.

Meanwhile they were waiting for us, and as I was to be the other that might be present with My Lord when he suffered, the priest and I went before him and behind the men-at-arms, while first went the Warden of the Castle. And we found that the scaffold had been put up upon a level with the window at the side of the main gate, which looks westward towards the City. There was a red cloth upon it, a square, but the rest naked, and round it a sort of railing of rope stretched from posts. The whole was guarded by soldiers of the King's Guard who were a-horse, even the drummers. There was a very great crowd of people who were silent, but when they saw My Lord shouted and made a confusion, till the soldiers pressed them back. The Warden asked My Lord whether he would speak to the people, but he shook his head and pressed his

lips together so firmly that one would have thought
he smiled. Then the Headsman, kneeling upon one
knee, as is the custom, asked My Lord's forgiveness
for what he was to do, to whom My Lord answered
in a cheerful voice that he very heartily forgave him
and all others in this matter. And then saying this
word "Come," wherein I did not understand his
meaning—but he may have been doing no more than
call me as one calls a servant—he took off his cloak,
which was dark and heavy and which was that which
he had commonly carried in the field, very service-
able and without ornament, and this cloak he handed
to me, so that I have it and will bring it with me
upon my journey. When he had done this he took
off also his undercoat, upon which, as upon his cloak,
he had kept no sign of his rank nor any jewel, even
of his Order; and this done he kissed me and also
him whom Your Excellency sent, the Religious; then
he knelt down and, as I think, prayed, but very
shortly, after which he laid his head upon the block
and asked the Headsman if it were fairly so. To
which the Headsman said yes, and that at his signal
he would strike: which, when it was given, the
Headsman struck, and by the mercy of God was
ready at his business: so we threw a cloth that had
been given us quickly over the body of My Lord,
and while the people groaned we lifted him, two
men-at-arms, the priest and I together, to set him
in a case of wood which was prepared. Only the
Headsman showed My Lord's head to the people,

A Secret Letter

and said, "So perish all traitors," while the people still groaned. Then My Lord's head also was given us and we set it very reverently down, and we covered the case with the cloth given us, which was the end of the business of that morning, from which time till now I have not written, but now write as Your Excellency ordered, and in the first hour in which I find myself able and in command of myself to do so.

My Lord was a great Captain.

THE SHADOWS

Iᴛ is always in a time when one's attention is at the sharpest strain, when innumerable details are separately and clearly grasped by the mind, and, in a word, when the external circumstance of life is most real to us that the comic contrast between ourselves and the greatness outside us can best be appreciated.

We humans make all that present which is never there, and which is always hurrying past us like the tumble of a stream, an all-important thing.

A form of dress unusual at one particularly insignificant moment, a form of words equally unusual, and so forth, seem like immovable eternities to us ; they seem so particularly in those moments when we are most thoroughly mixed with our time. Then what fun it is to remember that the whole thing, all the trappings of life, are nothing but a suit of clothes : old-fashioned almost before we have used them, and worthless anyhow.

It is a general election that has made me think these things.

In the moment of an election men mix together

very closely; the life of one's time is set before one
under a very brilliant and concentrated light, which
shows a thousand things one had forgotten in the
habits of the nation.

One sees so many kinds of men, one finds about
one the relics of so many philosophies, one is
astonished to meet, still surviving, so many illusions
—that these contemporary details take up a very
exaggerated place in our mind. Then it is good for
one to remember that the whole of it is but a little
smoke.

There are commonplace tags in history which boys
can never understand. One of the most commonplace and the most worn is Burke's exclamation in
the Bristol election. He heard of the death of a
man, and said : " What shadows we are, and what
shadows we pursue ! " and the phrase has gone
threadbare, and no school-boy can understand why
his elders dwell upon that phrase.

The reason is that it expresses a thing which is
not only obvious, but which also happens to be of
the utmost moment; and it is peculiarly valuable
coming from Burke, who of all men was keenest
upon the shams of his time, who of all men was most
immersed in the game of politics, who of all men,
perhaps, in Parliamentary history was capable of
self-deception and of the salaried advocacy which is
the basis of self-deception. Burke is, as it were, a
little god or idol of your true politician. He was a
politician of the politicians. Burke is to the politician

what Keats is to the poet, the exemplar, the mirror of the profession ; yet Burke it was who said : "What shadows we are, and what shadows we pursue ! " He was quite right.

A little time ago in Paris an experiment was tried, which later was repeated in London. It was a curious success in each capital. The experiment was this : to put upon the stage a play, the time of which was the sixties of the last century, and to dress the actors up in the clothes of the sixties. In Paris they went further : they reproduced the slang, the jests, the very tone and affectations of fashion which marked the period of Napoleon III. The younger generation, which could not remember the time, looked on curiously at the experiment. To the older people it was comic, with an uncanny comedy, and the irony of it was sometimes more bitter than they liked. So this was man ! This was the immortal being ! This was the ambitious fellow who would now write a deathless poem, now discover the ultimate truths of Hell and Heaven ; now dominate the earth with his machines, now enter the adventure of Mexico—and the rest ! There he was, in peg-top trousers, long whiskers, and an absurd top-hat with a narrow brim. And there was woman, the woman, for whom such and such a man had killed himself, such and such another had volunteered for the Crimea ; or the woman of whom a third had made a distant idol in the Atlas when he was out in Africa. And there was the woman upon whom the Court depended, or

The Shadows

the Ministry; there was the woman who had inspired the best work of Hugo, or who had changed the life of Renan. She wore a crinoline. At the back of her head was a mass of ugly false hair, and how odd these gestures seemed, and what queer turns of phrases there were in her language! What waxwork, and how dead the whole thing seemed!

That experiment in either capital was a dreadful one, which will not easily be tried again. Like all things that grip the mind, the power of its action lay in its truth, and the truth which vivified that experiment and gave it its power was the truth that our affairs are mortal things, and the ephemeral conditions which clothe our lives seem to us at a moment to be the universe itself, and yet are not even as important as the dust. They are small, they are ridiculously small—and also they are evanescent as the snow.

It is an amusement in which I have sometimes indulged, and no doubt many of those who are reading this have tried it for themselves, to turn to the files of old newspapers, choosing some period of great excitement which one can oneself remember, but which is separated from the present time by a sufficient space of years. It is well in practising this sport to choose the columns of a journal which expressed one's own enthusiasm and one's own conviction at the moment. The smile provoked by such a resurrection of the past must be bitter, but it will be the more salutary for its bitterness. *There* is that great question which (we supposed!) would change the world; *there* is all the shouting and the exaggeration and violence; and there, beyond it, unseen, is the reality which we have come to know. *Their* future has become *our* past, and note how utterly the vision disagrees with the real stuff, and see how vain the vision was. Look how terrors were never fulfilled, read how these hopes were still less destined to fulfilment, and, above all, attached to worthless ends.

In nothing is this lesson better learned or more valuable than in the matter of loves and hatreds. Look up the heroes. They were your heroes too. Read mournfully the enormous nonsense which was written of the villains. "Sir!" said a famous politician and writer of the Victorian time—"Sir! the world in which Palmerston is allowed to live makes me doubt the kindness of my Creator!" That is the kind of thing. Smith is your Hector and Jones is your Thersites! And then the mills of the years take up that flimsy stuff and begin grinding out reality, and what a different thing that finished article is from the raw material of guesswork and imagination with which the mills were fed! You can look back now and see the real Smith and the real Jones. You can see that the real Smith was chiefly remarkable for having one leg shorter than the other, and that the principal talent of the real Jones was the imitating of a steam engine, or a very neat way of playing cards; and that both Jones and Smith were of that common stature which men

The Shadows

have in the middle distance of a very ordinary
landscape.

For the benefit of mankind, the illusion which it
is impossible to feel with regard to a past actually
remembered re-arises when attached to a past longer
still. One can make a hero or villain of Fox or of
Pitt. One can look at the dress of the Eighteenth
Century, or the puffs and slashes of the Sixteenth,
not only without a smile, but actually with pleasure
and admiration. We find it glorious to read the
English of Elizabeth, and pleasant to read the plain
letters written when George the Third was King.
But, oh heavens! the Idylls of a King! I say, for
the benefit of man, one is allowed an illusion with
regard to the remote past; of the near past which
we have known, alas, we know the truth—and it
appals one with its emptiness. There is no doubt at
all that Burke was right for once in his life when he
said that we were shadows and that we pursued
shadows.

Nevertheless, there is one important thing, and
there is one eternal subject which survives.

THE CANVASSER

In that part of the Garden of Eden which lies somewhat to the south-west of the centre thereof the weather, during the recent election which was held there, was bad. It blew, it rained, it hailed, it snowed, and all this was on account of the great comet, of which the people of that region said proudly to strangers, " Have you seen our comet? " Imagining, with I know not how much justice, that this celestial phenomenon was local rather than national or imperial.

The Garden of Eden being mainly of a clay soil, large parts of it were flooded, and a Canvasser (a draper by profession and a Gentleman from London by birth), unacquainted as he was with the Garden of Eden, thought it a foul place, and picked his way without pleasure. He went down a lane the like of which he did not even know to exist in England (for it was what we call in the Garden of Eden a " green lane," and only those learned in the place could get along it at all during the floods).

I say he went down this lane, turned back, took a circumbendibus over some high but abominably

The Canvasser

sticky ploughed fields, and turned up with more of English earth than most citizens can boast at the door of the Important Cottage. He had been given his instructions carefully, and he was sure of the place. He swung off several pounds of clay from his boots to the right and to the left, and then it struck him that he did not know how to accost a cottage door. There was no knocker and there was no bell, But he had had plenty of proof and instruction dinned into him as to the importance of that cottage, so at last he made up his mind to do something bold and unconventional, and he knocked at it with his knuckles.

Hardly had he done so when he heard within a loud series of syllables proceeding from two human mouths and consisting mainly of the broad A in the vowels and of Z by way of the consonants. At last the door was opened a little way and a rather forbidding-looking old woman, short, fat, but energetic, looked out at him through the crack. She continued to look at him curiously, for it is good manners in the Garden of Eden to allow the guest to speak first.

When the Canvasser grasped this from the great length of silence which he had to endure, he said with the utmost politeness, taking off his hat in a graceful manner and speaking with the light accent of the cultured—

" Is your husband in, madam ? "

By way of answer she shut the door upon him and

disappeared, and the Canvasser, not yet angry, marvelled at the ways of the Garden of Eden. In a few moments she was back again; she opened the door a little wider, just wide enough to let him come in, and said—

"Ye can see un : but he bain't my husband. He wor my sister's husband like." As she said this she kept her eyes fixed upon the stranger, noting every movement of his face and of his body, until she got him into the large old kitchen. There she put a chair for him, and he sat down.

He found himself opposite a very, very old man, much older than the old woman, sitting in a patched easy chair and staring merrily but fixedly at the fire.

The very, very old man said : "Marnin'."

There was a pause. The Canvasser felt nervous. The old, fat, but energetic woman, still scowling somewhat and still fixedly regarding the stranger, said—

"I do be tellin' of un you bain't my husband, you be poor Martha's husband that was. Ar!"

"Ar!" said the old man, by way of corroboration; and the smile—if it were a smile—upon his drawn and wrinkled face became more mysterious than ever.

The Canvasser coughed a little. "I've brought bad weather with me," he said, by way of opening the delicate conversation.

"Ar!" said the old man. "You ain't brought un nayther! Naw . . . Bin ere a sennight com Vriday . . ." Then he added more reflectively, and as

106

though he were already passing into another world, while he stared at the fire : " You ain't brought un nayther ; naw ! "

" Well," said the stranger gallantly, though a little put out, " I'm sure I should have been sorry to have brought it."

" Ar, so you may zay ! Main sorry I lay," said the old man, and went off into a rattle of laughter which ended in a violent fit of coughing. But even as he coughed he wagged his head from side to side, relishing the joke immensely, and repeating it several times to himself in the intervals of his spasms.

" A lot of water lying about," said the Canvasser, hoping to start some vein at least which would lead somewhere.

" Mubbe zo, mubbe no," said the Ancient, like a true peasant, glancing sideways for the first time at his visitor and quickly withdrawing his eyes again. " Thur be mar watter zome plaa-ces nor others. . . . Zo they tell," he concluded, for fear of committing himself. Then he added : " I ain't bin out mesel'."

" He's got rheumatics chronic," said the sister-in-law, standing by and watching them both with equal disapproval.

" Ar ! " said the Ancient. " Arl ower me ! "

The Canvasser despaired. He took the plunge. He said as pleasantly as he could : " I've come to ask you how you're going to vote, Mr. Layton."

" Ow I be whaat ? " answered his host with a look of extreme cunning and affecting a sudden deafness as he put his left hand to his shrivelled ear and leaned towards the Londoner.

"How you were going to vote, Mr. Layton," said the Canvasser, still good-humoured, but a little more rosy than before, and leaning forward and speaking in a louder tone.

"Ow I were voattun?" answered the aged Layton with a touch of indignation in his cracked tones, "I ain't voättud 'tarl yet!"

"No, no, Mr. Layton," said the Canvasser, relieved at any rate to have got to the subject. "What I meant was how are you going to vote?"

"Oo! Ar!" quickly caught up the peasant. "If ye'd zed that furst orf, mebbe I'd a towd ee!" He gave another little cackle of laughter and looked into the fire.

"It is a very important election, Mr. Layton," said the Canvasser solemnly. "A great deal hangs on it."

"Doän you be worritin un, young man," said the sister-in-law with a touch of menace in her tone, her arms akimbo and her attitude sturdy.

"There do be zome," began the Ancient, absolutely off his own, and, so far as the bewildered Londoner could understand, entirely irrelevantly— "there do be zome as ave a bit of money lay by, an' there do be zome as as none. Ar! Them as as none kin do without un." He laughed again, this time rather unpleasantly, and more shortly than before.

There was an awkward silence. Then in a louder

voice and at a higher pitch he took up his tale again. " I mind my feythur saäying when I wor furst r'kmoinding, feythur says to me, 'Ar, you moind rooks and you get your farp'nce when Farmer Mouwen give it 'ee, and you bring it straäght whome t' me, zame as I tell ee.' "

This reminiscence concluded, the old man repeated his formula to the effect that there were some who had money laid by, others who had none, and that those who had none would have to do without that commodity. Of this sentiment his sister-in-law, by a slight nod, expressed her full approval. Her lips were firmer set than ever, and she was positively glaring at her guest.

The Canvasser began to shift uneasily. " Well, I put it straight, Mr. Layton," he said—" will you vote for Mr. Richards ? "

" Ar ! Ye can putt un straäght," answered the Ancient, with a look of preternatural cunning, " and ah can answer un straäght, an wow ! ye'd be none wiser. . . . Ar ! reckon t' answer any man straäght 's any man there be erebouts, naabur, nor no naabur ! And zo I tell un."

" That's right," said his sister-in-law, approvingly, " and so e tell 'ee ! " She was beginning to look actually threatening, but the Canvasser had not yet got his answer.

" We really do hope that we can hear you are going to vote for Mr. Richards." he said pleadingly. " The action of the Government——"

On Anything

" Ar, zo I do ear say," said the old man, chuckling over some profound thought. " And Mas'r Willum e do zay thaät too, though e be tother side." He wagged his head twice with the wise subtlety of age. " Ar now, which way be I going to voät? Ar? Thaät's what many on us ud like t' know!"

The Canvasser began to despair. He kept his weary smile upon his face, rose from his chair, and said: " Well, I must be going now, madam."

" That ye must," said the old lady cheerfully.

" Don't you let un go wi'out gi'ing un some of that wa-ine," said the host, as he leaned forward in his chair and stirred the down fire with an old charred stick.

The woman looked at the Canvasser suspiciously and poured him out some parsnip wine, which he drank with the best grace in the world. As he lifted the glass he said, with an assumed cheerfulness: " Well! here's to Mr. Richards!"

" Ar!" said the old man.

The old woman took the glass, wiped it carefully without washing it, put it back into the cupboard with the bottle, and turned round to continue her occupation of fixing the stranger with her eye.

" Well, I must be gone," he said for the second time, and in as breezy a tone as he could command.

" Ar, zo you zay!" was all the reply he obtained, and he left that citizen of many years still smiling with his bony aged jaws at the down fire, and muttering again to himself that great truth about

110

The Canvasser

material wealth which had haunted him throughout the brief conversation.

The woman shut the door behind the Canvasser, and he was off across the fields. In the next cottage he came to he asked them which way old Layton would vote. The woman at the place answered nothing, but her son, a very tall and silent young man with a soft nascent beard, who was stacking wood to the leeward of the house, smiled secretly and said—

" Ar ! "

THE ABSTRACTED MAN

I HAD occasion the other day to catch a train which was going to the West of England from Paddington, and I was in a taxi, which was open because the weather was clear.

Now when we came to within about a quarter of a mile of Paddington we got into a block, which was exasperating in the extreme, for my time was short, and immediately in front of me, also in an open taxi —an astonishing thing, and one I had never seen before—sat a man who though all alone yet had his back to the driver. Even in the rush of the moment I could not help being fixed and somewhat stirred by his face. It was a face of intense weariness, yet in it there was a sort of patient rest. He had a thin, straggling beard, so thin that it was composed, as it were, of separate hairs ; his eyes were very hollow and long-drawn, and his eyebrows arched unduly, as though on some occasion in his life—long past and by this time half forgotten—he had suffered some immense surprise.

The expression in those eyes was one of unchangeable but meek sadness. He had a high-domed forehead, as some poets have, and he wore upon it, tilted rather far back, a dirty grey hat, soft and somewhat on one side. He had a heavy old grey overcoat upon him. He was thin. He had no gloves upon his hands, which were long and bony and very withered. These hands of his were clasped one over the other upon the handle of his umbrella. So he sat, and so I watched him; I in a fever to catch a train, he apparently no longer fighting the complexities of this world.

The block broke up and we all began to dodge past each other towards Paddington. His taxi turned into the station just in front of mine. We got out together. I was interested to note that he asked for a ticket to the same station in the same town which I was about to visit. So great was my curiosity that I did what perhaps no one should do save a servant of the State in pursuit of a criminal, that is, I deliberately watched into which carriage he got and I got in with him. The express started and we were alone together for some two hours. He sat in the opposite corner to mine, still patient and still silent. He had bought no newspaper, his hands were still clasped on his umbrella, and he looked out of the window without interest as we passed by the various degrees of sordid and unhappy life which fringe London. And when we came out into the open country he still continued to gaze thus emptily.

I was most eager to speak to him, but I did not know how to begin. He solved the difficulty for

I

me by saying at a point where the great mass of Windsor is to be seen to the south of the line upon a clear day (and he leant forward to say it and said it in a low, rather pleading voice): "Stands out well?"

"Yes," said I.

"Stands out wonderful well!" he said again, and sighed, not profoundly, but in a manner that was very touching to hear.

When a little while later we crossed the Thames he moved his head slowly to look down at the water, and he sighed as we passed the town of Maidenhead. Then he said to me again spontaneously, "D'you often travel upon this line?"

I said I travelled upon it fairly often, and I asked him, since this appeared to strike some slight note of interest in his mind, whether he travelled upon it also. He answered, in a tone a little lower and sadder than that which he had used before and shaking his poor grey head from side to side. "Not now!... I did once.... But it was broad gauge then!" and again he sighed profoundly.

He continued upon this topic, which apparently had been one of the thin veins of interest in the mine of his heart. He told me they would never have anything like the old broad gauge again—never; and he shook his head pathetically once more. He proceeded to remember the name of Isambard Brunel, and he spoke of the Thames Tunnel and how men could go dry shod under the river. "Under the

The Abstracted Man

river! Dry shod from one shore to the other! Marvellous. . . ."

Then, still on that theme, he referred to the *Great Eastern* and said what a mighty great ship she was.

"They will never have another like her—never! No one else will ever make a ship as big as that!'

Now at this point I would have contradicted him had I known him to be a man upon whom contradiction might act as a tonic and he might have told me something about his extraordinary self. For it is certain that now-a-days ships much larger than the *Great Eastern* and fifty times more efficient sail in and out of our harbours every hour. And I could even have told him that the *Great Eastern* had been broken up—but I did not know that such a truth might not provoke tears in those old eyes, so I forbore.

After a little pause he continued again, for he was now fairly on the run: "Wonderful thing—steam!" and then he was silent for a long while.

I began to wonder whether perhaps he was much older than I had guessed, but in a little while he settled this for me by talking to me with some enthusiasm of Lord Palmerston. It was an enthusiasm of youth. I know not how many metaphors he did not use. Little bits of sly slang—as dead as the pyramids—peeped into his conversation as he described his hero, and he would always end a paragraph of his panegyric by wagging his head and letting his heart sink again at the reflection that such men could not endure for ever.

I gently agreed with him and talked boastfully of foreign politics (for that was the trend of his own mind apparently), but his ideas upon these were not only simple but few. He had a craze that made it very difficult to keep up, if I may use that expression, for his one obsession was the French; and though he was too patriotic to prophesy their arrival upon these shores his head shook more nervously than ever when he had turned on to that topic. However, he said, we had beaten them before and we should beat them again; and he added that it was not the same Napoleon. His mind fastened upon this relief and he repeated it several times. Then he remained silent for a while, too tired to notice the towns among which we were passing.

I asked him whether he was acquainted with the Vale of the White Horse. He told me sadly, and with the first faint smile I had seen upon his face, that he had known it years ago, but "not now." He said that when he had known it the White Horse was much more distinct and much more like a horse, and he wandered on to tell me that Swindon to-day was not at all the place it had been. This was his universal judgment of everything along the line, and for a little he would have told me that the crest of the downs had changed.

He remarked that there was no wheat in the fields, which, after all, was not surprising at this time of year, and looking at the dull earth as we passed it he assured me he could remember the time when the whole of it had been yellow with corn, and if I had said: "But not in January?" I might have compelled him to an uneasy silence, which was the last thing in the world I wished.

Perhaps what I most remarked about him as strange was his not reading. I have already said that he had bought no newspaper for himself, but he did not ask for mine. When his eyes fell upon it where it lay upon the seat they looked at it as a man looks at the cat upon the hearthrug. But he did not take up the paper, though the moment through which we were passing was not without interest—and this leads me to the way in which we parted.

We had sat for some time in silence, his old face still turned to the rapid landscape, which took on with every mile more and more the unmistakable nature of the West of England, the sharp hills, the combes, and with it all that which has something about it *Roman*, a note I never miss when I cross its boundaries. At lást we drew up into the great station of the city. I opened the door for him and got out first in case he should wish to hand me his bag. But though he was feeble he took it down himself and slowly came out of the carriage backwards and with the utmost caution; when he reached the platform he gasped, with some little hint of adventure in his tone, "There!" And he told me

On Anything

that railways were dangerous things. So we went down the platform together, for I wished to get all the experience of him I could before we had to part. He knew his way out, and when we got into the main place of the town an enormous mob, pushing and shoving, cheering and doing all that mobs do, was filling the whole of it. For the first time since we had met I saw a look of terror in his old eyes. He whispered to me, instead of speaking, "What's all that?"

"It's only a crowd," I said. "They're good-natured enough. It's the election."

"The election?" he answered, his look of terror increasing. "Whose election? Oh, I never could abide a riot! I never could abide one!"

I assured him I would get him through without any danger, and I took his thin arm in mine, and pushed and scrambled him through to a hotel that was near and there I left him. The terror had left his eyes, but he was much weaker. I asked him if I could do anything more, but the manageress told me that she knew him and that he often came there. She was a very capable person, and she reassured me, and so I left the Abstracted Man, he telling me in a tone still low, but no longer in a whisper, that he dursen't go out until the riot was gone.

And all this shows that during an election you meet more different kinds of men and explore more corners of England than at any other time. Not

118

The Abstracted Man

until I had lost him did I remember that I had
forgotten to ask him on which side of our present
struggle he had formed his opinion, but perhaps
it was just as well I did not. It would only have
confused him.

ON THE METHOD OF HISTORY

An apprehension of the past demands two kinds of information.

First, the mind must grasp the inner nature of historic change, and therefore must be made acquainted with the conditions of human thought in each successive period, as also with the general scheme of its revolution.

Secondly, the external actions of men, the sequence in dates and hours of such actions, and their material conditions and environment must be strictly and accurately acquired.

Neither of these two foundations, upon which repose both the teaching and the learning of history, is more important than the other. Each is essential. But a neglect of the due emphasis which one or the other demands, though both be present, warps the judgment of the scholar and forbids him to apply this science to its end, which is the establishment of truth.

History may be called the test of true philosophy, or it may be called in a very modern and not very dignified metaphor the object-lesson of political science, or it may be called the great story whose

On the Method of History

interest is upon another plane from all other stories because its irony, its tragedy, and its moral are real, were acted by real men, and were the manifestation of God.

Whatever brief and epigrammatic summary we make to explain the value of history to men, that formula still remains an imperative formula for them all, and I repeat it : the end of history is the establishment of truth.

A man may be ever so accurately informed as to the dates, the hours, the weather, the gestures, the type of speech, the very words, the soil, the colour, that between them all would seem to build up a particular event. But if he be not seized of the mind which lay behind all that was human in the business, then no synthesis of his detailed knowledge is possible. He cannot give to the various actions which he knows their due order and proportion ; he knows not what to omit, nor what to enlarge upon among so many, or rather a number potentially infinite of, facts ; and his picture will not be (as some would put it) distorted : it will be false. He will not be able to use history for its end, which is the establishment of Truth. All that he establishes by his action, and all that he confirms and makes stronger, is Untruth. And so far as truth is concerned it would be far better that a man should be possessed of no history than that he should be possessed of history ill-stated as to its prime factor, which is human motive.

121

On Anything

A living man has, to aid his judgment and to guide him in the establishment of truth, contemporary experience. Other men are his daily companions. The consequence and the living principles of their acts and of his own are fully within his grasp. If he is rightly informed of all the past motive and determining mind from which the present has sprung, that information of his will illumine and expand and confirm his use of present experience. If he know nothing of the past his personal observation and the testimony of his own senses are, so far as they go, an unshakable foundation. But if he brings to the aid of contemporary experience an appreciation of the past which is false because it gives to the past a mind which was not its own, then he will not only be wrong upon that past, but he will tend to be wrong also in his conclusions upon the present. He will for ever read into the plain facts before him origins and predetermining forces which do not explain them and which are not connected with them in the way he imagines. He will come to regard his own society —which, as a man wholly uninstructed, he might fairly though insufficiently have grasped—through a veil of illusion and of false philosophy, until at last he will not even be able to see the things before his eyes. In a word, it is better to have no history at all than to have history which misconceives what were the general direction and the large sweeps of thought in the immediate and the remoter past.

On the Method of History

This being evidently the case, one is tempted to say that a just estimate of the revolution and the progression of human motive in the past is everything to history, and that an accurate scholarship in the details of the chronicle, in dates especially, is of wholly inferior importance. Such a statement would be quite false. Scholarship in history (that is, an acquaintance with the largest possible number of facts, and an accurate retention of them in the memory) is as essential to this study as is that other background of motive which has just been examined.

The thing is self-evident if we put an extreme case. For if a man were wholly ignorant of the facts of history and of their sequence, he could not possibly know what might lie behind the actions of the past, for we only obtain communion with that which is within and that which is foundational in human action by an observation of its external effect. A man's history, for instance, is sound and on the right lines if, though he have but a vague and general sentiment of the old pagan civilisation of the Mediterranean, that sentiment corresponds to the very large outline and is in sympathy with the main spirit of the affair. But he cannot possess so much as a sketch of the truth if he has not heard the names of certain of the great actors, if he is wholly unacquainted with the conception of a City State, and if the names of Rome, of Athens, of Antioch, of Alexander, and of Jerusalem have never been mentioned to him.

On Anything

Nor will a knowledge of facts be valuable (contrariwise, it will be detrimental and of negative value to his judgment), if accuracy in his knowledge be lacking. If he were invariably inaccurate, thinking that red which was blue, inverting the order of any two events, and putting without fail in the summer what happened in winter, or in the Germanies what took place in Gaul, his facts would never correspond with the human motive of them, and his errors upon externals would at once close his avenues of access towards internal motive and suggest other and non-existent motive in its place.

It is, of course, a pedantic and negligible error to imagine that the knowledge of a time grows out of a mere accumulation of observation. External things do not produce ideas, they only reveal them. And to imagine that mere scholarship is sufficient to history is to put one's self on a level with those who, in the sphere of politics for instance, ignore the necessity of political theory and talk muddily of the " working" of institutions—as though it were possible to judge whether an institution were working ill or not when one had no ideal of what that institution might be designed to attain. But though scholarship is not the source of judgment in history, it is the invariable and the necessary accompaniment of it. Facts which (to repeat) do not produce ideas, but only reveal or suggest them, do none the less reveal and suggest them, and form the only instrument of such suggestion and revelation.

124

On the Method of History

Scholarship, accurate and widespread, has this further function : that it is necessary to a general apprehension of the past, which, however just, is the firmer, the larger, and the more intense as the range of knowledge and its fixity increase. And scholarship has one more function, which is that it corrects, and it corrects with more and more precision in proportion as it is more and more detailed, the tendency of the mind to extend a general and perhaps justly apprehended idea into the region of unreality. For the mind is creative ; it will still make and spin ; and if you do not feed it with material it will spin dreams out of emptiness. Thus a man will have a just appreciation of the Thirteenth Century in England, he will perhaps admirë or will perhaps be repelled by its whole spirit according to his temperament or his acquired philosophy ; but in either case, though his general impression was once just, he will, if he considers it apart from reading, tend to add to it excrescences of judgment, which, as the process continues, will at last destroy the true image ; scholarship, like a constant auditor, comes in regularly to check and tally his conclusions. Does he admire the Thirteenth Century ? Then he will tend to make it more national than it was because our time is national, and to forget its cruelties because the good enthusiasms of our own age happen for the moment not to be accompanied by cruelty. He will tend to lend the Thirteenth Century a science it did not possess, because physical science is in our own

On Anything

time an accompaniment of greatness. But if he reads and reads continually, these vagaries will not oppress or warp his vision. More and more body will be added to that spirit which he does justly, but only vaguely, know. And he will at last have with the English Thirteenth Century something of that acquaintance which one has with a human face and voice : these also are external things, and these also are the product of a soul. Indeed—though metaphors are dangerous in such a matter—a metaphor may with reservation be used to describe the effect of the chronicle, of research, and of accurate scholarship in the science of history. A man ill provided with such material is like one who sees a friend at a distance ; a man well provided with it is like a man who sees a friend close at hand. Both are certain of the identity of the person seen, both are well founded in that certitude ; but there are errors possible to the first which are not possible to the second, and close and intimate acquaintance lends to every part of judgment a surety which distant and general acquaintance wholly lacks. The one can say something true and say it briefly : there is no more to say. The other can fill in and fill in the picture, until though perhaps never complete it is a symptotic to completion.

To increase one's knowledge by research, to train one's self to an accurate memory of it, does not mean that one's view of the past is continually changing. Only a fool can think, for instance, that

On the Method of History

some document somewhere will be discovered to show that the mass of the people of London had for James II an ardent veneration, or that the national defence organised by the Committee of Public Safety during the French Revolution was due to the unpopular tyranny of a secret society. But research in either of these cases, and a minute and increasing acquaintance with detail, does show one a London largely apathetic in the first case, and does show one large sections of rebellious feeling in the armies of the Terror. It permits one to appreciate what energy and what initiative were needed for the overthrow of the Stuarts, and to see from how small a body of wealthy and determined men that policy proceeded. It permits one to understand how the battles of '93 could never have been fought upon the basis of popular enthusiasm alone ; it permits one to assert without exaggeration that the autocratic power of the Committee of Public Safety and the secrecy of its action were necessary conditions of the national defence during the French Revolution.

One might conclude by saying what might seem too good to be true : that minute and accurate information upon details (the characteristic of our time in the science of history) must of its own nature so corroborate the just and general judgments of the past that when the modern phase of wilful distortion is over mere blind scholarship will restore tradition.

ON HISTORY IN TRAVEL

I HAVE sometimes wondered whether it might not be possible to have guide-books written for the great routes of modern travel—I mean of modern pleasure-travel—which should make the whole road a piece of history; for history enlarges everything one sees, and gives a fulness to flat experience, so that one lives more than one's own life in contemplating it, and so that new landscapes are not only new for a moment, but subject to centuries of varieties in one's mind.

It is true that those who write good guide-books do put plenty of history into them, but it is sporadic history, as it were ; it is not continuous or organic, and therefore it does not live.   You are told of a particular town that such was its Roman name ; that centuries later such a mediæval contest was decided in its neighbourhood.   If it is connected in some way with the military history of this country you will be given some detailed account of an action fought there, and that is particularly the case in Spain, which one leaves with the vague impression that it was created to serve as a terrain for the Peninsular War.

On History in Travel

All knowledge of that sort interests the traveller, but it hardly remains, nor does it " inform " in the full sense of that word. Now, to be " informed " is the object, and the process of it is the pleasure, of learning. To give life to the history of places there must be connection in it, and it so happens that with *our* travel to-day—especially our pleasure-travel—a connection stands ready to the writer's hand : for we go in herds to-day along the great roads which have made Europe. It is the railways that have done this. Before they were built the network of cross-roads — already excellent in the end of the Eighteenth Century and the beginning of the Nineteenth—tempted men of leisure in every direction ; towns that had something curious to show were visited as easily, whether they lay on the main roads or no. The fruit of that time you may see in the great inns which still stand, though often half deserted, in places eccentric to modern travel. It may be that this old universality of travel will return with our new ease of going wherever there is a good surface for wheels—it has in part returned —but still much the most of us go along the lines laid down fast for us by the first great expenditure upon railways, and this was invested, necessarily, along some at least of the immemorial tracks which —from long before history—were the framework of Western society.

If you are from the North and go to the Riviera— from thence on, down the coast to Rome, you go mile for mile along the central highway that bound together the Roman Empire, the road that Hadrian went and Constantine descended. York, London, Dover, Boulogne, Laon, Dijon, Lyons, Marseilles are the posts strung along it, and the same long line is the line of advance which the Creed took when Christianity came up northwards from the Mediterranean. It is the line the second advent of that influence took when St. Augustine brought it back to this island after the breakdown of the Empire. Or if you will consider that short eight hours of tearing speed which so many thousands know, the main line from London to Paris, see what a thick past there is gathered all along it. The crossing of the Darent, where stood one of the string of Canterbury palaces, and just to the left of your train the field where Edmund Ironside met the Danes, further on Wrotham, another of the archbishops' line of houses, and on the hills above and in the plain below the sacred monoliths that the savages put up for worship before letters or buildings were known, and beyond the valley Kit's Coty House and the bare place where stood the Rood of Boxley and Aylesford, the first bridge where the pirates first drove the British in their conquest of this country, and much further the British camp which the Tenth Legion stormed, standing above the Stour. Canterbury, where there is fixed continuity with Rome and with the history before Rome, the little Roman bricks in St. Martin's Church, the Roman roads radiating to the ports of the Channel, and the British tracks on which they lay or which they straightened, deep under the site of the city the group of lake-dwellings when its defence was a lagoon, now meads—and, in the site of the great Central Tower, the end of the Middle Ages with which that town is crammed. Or if you reach it by the northern way, then everywhere you are following the great military road whereby for two thousand years travel has come from the Straits to London; Rochester, the armed defence of the river-crossing, the capture of whose castle twice gave an army the South of England, and all but saved Henry III against his Barons; the second bishopric of England; the garrison which stood central and sheltered the halt of forced marches from the sea upon London—and every step of the way Chaucer.

If you cross by Boulogne you see above you, on the last of English land, the hill forts they built to overlook the broad shallow harbour of Lemanus, now dry; you cross upon the narrow sea the track of Cæsar, who, when he first invaded, drifted here under a light breeze and with the tide for hours, coming with the transports from Boulogne and beaching at last upon the flats of Deal. Also in Boulogne that broad valley was a land-locked harbour in Cæsar's day, and there he built his ships.

If you cross by Calais you come, some three miles from French land, over that good holding ground where the Armada lay at anchor on a summer evening waiting to take aboard the unconquered soldiery which was designed for the assault of England ; but Howard and the flock of little English boats came up after, just thwart of Griz-nez, which you see tall and huge to your right : they lay there at anchor out of range against the stormy sunset, and when night came drove in their fire-ships against the Spanish Fleet and broke its formation, and next day the tempest drove them up that flat coast to your left, and so on to destruction in the open sea.

Then see how the French road is full also. Here, just beyond Etaples, is the place where the two ambassadors passed in '93, neither knowing the other : the one returning, driven out of London, the other posting thither at full speed to avert war. They missed, and so war came. A little further on to your left is a patch of wood; to your right, beyond the flats, is a broad estuary of which you may see the lighthouse towers. That wood is the wood of Crécy : through it there marched the English host on their way to victory in the rising ground beyond. The river mouth is that whence William started with his hundreds of ships on the way to Hastings : he lay gathered there with the wind in his teeth for days, until the equinox sent him a south-wester and he bowled across to Pevensey and landed there : every stretch of this road is alive with stories and things done.

The way down into Italy by Bourg is a way of armies also, though not a way of English armies, and it is a way of great influences too. Thus, if you would see the Gothic North and the Southern Renaissance first meeting, like salt water and fresh at the turn of a river-tide, get out at Bourg and drive a mile to Brou and see there the tombs of the House of Savoy. There is no sight like it in Europe, yet how few know it out of all who whirl down that line—often by night—on the way to the Alps or to Italy?

There are other roads: each tempts one to a list of wonders. The road northeastward from Paris, every step of which is the line of the last Napoleonic struggle. The road eastward into Germany by Metz, every step of which is the history of the Revolution, or of invasion, or of success in the field. A little station which your eyes will hardly catch as the express goes by is neighbour to the camp that Attila made before he was defeated in those plains of Champagne; another little station, the station of a hidden hamlet, is called Valmy; half-an-hour on, beyond Les Islettes, you see quite close by the forest path that Drouet took when he intercepted the flight of the King and so destroyed the French Monarchy.

All these roads are known roads, but there is one which the railway has abandoned and which is therefore half derelict; many motors rediscover it, for it has half the story of Europe strung along it—I mean the road from Paris by Tours and Poictiers to Perigueux, to Toulouse, over the High Pyrenees and

On Anything

on to Saragossa. No one line serves it. Across the mountains for a day and more of travel there is no line at all, but this is the road up which Islam came a thousand years ago to end us. The host got past Poictiers. Charles met them from Tours and they were destroyed. You may see the place to-day, and this is the road by which all the Frankish and Gothic invasions moved on Spain, and this is the road that Charlemagne must have taken when he first marched across the hills against the Valley of Ebro. I know of no road more holy with past wars, none more wonderful where it meets the mountains, none better made for all sorts of going—and none more deserted than it is upon the high places between France and Spain—but of this road I will write later to prove how much there may be in travel.

ON THE TRAVELLER

THOSE who travel about England for their pleasure, or, for that matter, about any part of Western Europe, rightly associate with such travel the pleasure of history : for history adds to a man, giving him, as it were, a great memory of things like a human memory, but stretched over a far longer space than that of one human life. It makes him, I do not say wise and great, but certainly in communion with wisdom and greatness.

It adds also to the soil he treads, for to this it adds meaning. How good it is when you come out of Tewkesbury by the Cheltenham road, to look upon those fields to the left and know that they are not only pleasant meadows, but also the place in which the fate of English mediæval monarchy was decided ; or, as you stand by that ferry which is not known enough to Englishmen (for it is one of the most beautiful things in England) and look back and see Tewkesbury tower framed between tall trees over the level of the Severn, to see the Abbey buildings in your eye of the mind—a great mass of similar stone with solid Norman walls, standing to the right of the building.

135

On Anything

All this historical sense and the desire to marry History with Travel is very fruitful and nourishing, but there is another interest allied to it which is very nearly neglected, and which is yet in a way more fascinating and more full of meaning. This interest is the interest in such things as lie behind recorded history, and have survived into our own times. For underneath the general life of Europe, with its splendid epic of great Rome turned Christian, crusading, discovering, furnishing the springs of the Renaissance and flowering at last materially into this stupendous knowledge of to-day, the knowledge of all the Arts, the power to construct and to do— underneath all that is the foundation on which Europe is built, the stem from which Europe springs; and that stem is far, far older than any recorded history, and far, far more vital than any of the phenomena which recorded history presents.

Recorded history for this island, and for Northern France and for the Rhine Valley, is a matter of two thousand years; for the Western Mediterranean of three; but the things of which I speak are to be reckoned in tens of thousands of years. Their interest does not lie only or even chiefly in things that disappeared. It is indeed a great pleasure to rummage in the earth and find the polished stones of the men who came so many centuries before us, but of whose blood we certainly are; and it is a great pleasure to find or to guess that we find under Canterbury the piles of a lake or marsh dwelling,

On the Traveller

proving that Canterbury has been there from all time, and that the apparently defenceless valley city was once chosen as an impregnable site when the water-meadows of the Stour were impassable as marsh, or with difficulty passable as a shallow lagoon. And it is delightful to stand on the earthwork beyond Chilham and to say to oneself (as one can say with a fair certitude), "Here was the British camp defending the south-east; here the tenth legion charged." All these are pleasant, but more pleasant I think to follow the thing where it actually survives.

Consider the Track-ways, for instance. How rich England is in these! No other part of Europe will afford the traveller so permanent and so fascinating a problem. Elsewhere Rome hardened and straightened every barbaric trail, but in this distant province of Britain she would only spend just so much energy as made them a foothold for her soldiery; and all over England you go if you choose foot by foot along the ancient roads that were made by the men of your blood before they had heard of brick, or of stone, or of iron, or of written laws.

I wonder that more men do not set out to follow, let us say, the Fosse-way. There it runs right across Western England from the south-west to the north-east, in a line direct yet sinuous, characters which are the very essence of a savage trail. It is a modern road for many miles, let us say; and there

137

you are tramping along the Cotswold on a hard-metalled modern English highway, with milestones and notices from the county council telling you that the culverts will not bear a steam-engine, if so be you were travelling in one. Then suddenly it comes up against a cross-road and apparently ceases, making what map draughtsmen call a "T"; but right in the same line you will see a gate, and beyond it a farm lane, and so you follow. You come to a spinney where a ride is cut through by the wood-reeve, and it is all in the same line. The Fosse-way turns into a little path, but you are still on it; it curls over a marshy brook-valley, keeping on firm land, and as you go you see old stones put there Heaven knows how many generations ago—or perhaps yesterday, for the tradition remains and the countryfolk strengthen their wet lands as they have strengthened them all these thousands of years; you climb up out of that depression, you get you over a stile, and there you are again upon a lane. You follow that lane, and once more it stops dead. This time there is a field before you. No right of way, no trace of a path, nothing but grass rounded into those parallel ridges which mark the decay of the corn lands and pasture taking the place of agriculture. Now your pleasure comes in casting about for the trail; you look back along the line of the way; you look forward in the same line till you find some indication, a boundary between two parishes, perhaps upon your map, or two or three quarries set together, or some other sign; and very soon you have picked up the line again.

So you go on mile after mile, and as you tread that line you feel in the horizons that you see, in the very nature and feel of the soil beneath your feet, in the skies of England above you, the ancient purpose and soul of this kingdom. Up this same line went the Clans marching when they were called Northward to the Host; and up this went slow, creaking wagons with the lead of the Mendips or the tin of Cornwall, or the gold of Wales.

And it is still there; it is still used from place to place as a high-road, it still lives in modern England. There are some of its peers: as for instance the Ermine Street, far more continuous, and affording problems more rarely; others like the ridgeway of the Berkshire Downs, which Rome hardly touched, and of which the last two thousand years has therefore made hardly anything. You may spend a delightful day piecing out exactly where it crossed the Thames, making your guess at it, and wondering as you sit there by Streatley Vicarage whether those islands did not form a natural weir below which lay the ford.

The roads are the most obvious things. There are many more; for instance, thatch. The same laying of the straw in the same manner, with the same art, has continued, we may be certain, from a time long before the beginning of history. See how in the Fen Land they thatch with reeds, and how upon the Chalk Downs with straw from the lowlands. I remember once being told of a record in a manor which held of the church, and which lay upon the southern slope of the Downs, that so much was entered " for straw from the lowlands "; then years afterwards, when I had to thatch a Bethlehem in an orchard underneath tall elms—a pleasant place to write in with the noise of bees in the air—the man who came to thatch said to me : " We must have straw from the lowlands ; this upland straw is no good for thatching." Then immediately when I heard him say this there was added to me ten thousand years. And I know another place in England, far distant from this, where a man said to me that if I wished to cross in a winter mist, as I had determined to do, Cross Fell, that great summit of the Pennines, I must watch the drift of the snow, for there was no other guide to one's direction in such weather. And I remember another man in a boat in the North Sea, as we came towards the Foreland, talking to me of the two tides, and telling me how if one caught the tide all the way up to Long Nose and then went round it, one made two tides in one day. He spoke with the same pleasure that silly men show when they talk about an accumulation of money. He felt wealthy and proud from the knowledge, for by this knowledge he had two tides in one day. Now knowledge of this sort is older than ten thousand years ; and so is the knowledge of how birds fly, and of how they call, and of how the weather changes with the moon.

On the Traveller

Very many things a man might add to the list that I am making. Dew-pans are older than our language or religion; and the finding of water with a stick; and the catching of that difficult animal, the mole; and the building of flints into mortar, which if one does it the old way (as you may see at Pevensey) lasts for ever, and if you do it the new way does not last ten years; and then there is the knowledge of planting during the crescent part of the month but not before the new moon shows; and there is the influence of the moon on cider, and to a less extent upon the brewing of ale; and talking of ale, the knowledge of how ale should be drawn from the brewing just when a man can see his face without mist upon the surface of the hot brew; and there is the knowledge of how to bank rivers, which is called "throwing the rives" in the South, but in the Fen Land by some other name; and how to bank them so they do not silt, but scour themselves. There are these things and a thousand others. All are immemorial, but I have no space for any now.

ON MILTON

THE letters of a people reflect its noblest as architecture reflects its most intimate mind and as its religion (if it has a separate or tribal religion) reflects its military capacity or incapacity. The word " noblest " is vague, and nobility must here be defined to mean that steadiness in the soul by which it is able to express a fixed character and individuality of its own. Thus a man contradicts himself from passion or from a variety of experience or from the very ambiguity and limitation of words, but he himself resides in all he says, and when this self is clearly and poisedly expressed it is then that we find him noble.

The poet Milton, according to this conception, has best expressed the nobility of the English mind, and in doing a work quite different from any of his peers has marked a sort of standard from which the ideal of English letters does not depart.

Two things are remarkable with regard to English literature, first that it came late into the field of European culture, and secondly that it has proved extraordinarily diversified. The first point is imma-

On Milton

terial to my subject; the second is material to it;
for it might be superficially imagined that such
bewildering complexity and, as it were, lawless
exuberance of method and of matter would never
find a pole, nor ever be symbolised by but one aspect
of it. Yet Milton has found that pole, and Milton's
work has afforded that symbol.

In any one moment of English literary history you
may contrast two wholly different masterpieces from
the end of the Fourteenth to the end of the
Eighteenth Centuries. After the first third of the
Nineteenth, indeed, first-rate work falls into much
more commonplace groove, and it is perceptible that
the best verse and the best prose written in English
are narrowing in their vocabulary, and, in what is far
more important, their way of looking at life. The
newspapers have levelled the writers down as with a
trowel; you have not side by side the coarse and the
refined, the amazing and the steadfast, the grotesque
and the terrible; but in all those earlier centuries
you had side by side manner and thought so varied
that a remote posterity will wonder how such a
wealth could have arisen upon so small an area of
national soil. *Piers Plowman* and the *Canterbury
Tales* are two worlds, and a third world separate
from each is the world of those lovely lyrics which
are now so nearly forgotten, but which the populace
spontaneously engendered and sang throughout the
close of the Middle Ages. The Sixteenth Century
was perhaps less modulated, and flowed, especially

towards its end, in one simpler stream, but in the Seventeenth what a growth of variety from the Jacobean translation of the Bible to Swift. The very decade in which *Paradise Lost* was published corresponded with the first riot of the Restoration.

If we look closely into all this diversity we can find two common qualities which mark out all English work in a particular manner from the work of other nations. To qualities of this kind, which are like colours rather than like measurable things, it is difficult to give a title; I will hazard, however, these two words, "Adventure" and "Mystery." There is no English work of any period, especially is there no English work of any period later than the middle of the Sixteenth Century, which has not got in it all those emotions which proceed from the love of Adventure. How notable it is, for instance, that Landscape appears and reappears in every diverse form of English verse. Even in Shakespeare you have it now and then as vivid as a little snapshot, and it runs unceasingly through every current of the stream; it glows in Gray's *Elegy*, and it is the binding element of *In Memoriam*. It saves the earlier work of Wordsworth, it permeates the large effect of Byron, and those two poems, which to-day no one reads, *Thalaba* and *The Curse of Kehama*, are alive with it. It is the very inspiration of Keats and of Coleridge. Now this hunger for Landscape and this vivid sense of it are but aspects of Adventure; for the men who thus feel and

speak are the men who, desiring to travel to
unknown places, are in a mood for sudden revela-
tions of sea and land.   So a living poet has written—

> When all the holy primal part of me
> Arises up within me to salute
> The glorious vision of the earth and sea
> That are the kindred of the destitute . . . .

The note of those four lines is the note of Landscape in English letters, and that note is the best
proof and effect of Adventure.   If any man is too
poor to travel (though I cannot imagine any man so
poor), or if he is constrained from travel by the
unhappy necessities of a slavish life, he can always
escape through the door of English letters.   Let
such a one read the third and fourth books of
Paradise Lost before he falls asleep and he will
find next morning that he has gone on a great
journey.   Milton by his perpetual and ecstatic
delight in these visions of the world was the normal
and the central example of an English poet.

> As when far off at sea a fleet descri'd
> Hangs in the clouds . . . .

or, again,

> . . . . Hesperus, that led
> The Starry Host, rode brightest 'til the Moon,
> Rising in cloudy majesty, at length
> Apparent Queen, unveiled . . . .

He everywhere, and in a profusion that is, as it
were, rebellious against his strict discipline of words,
sees and expresses the picture of this world.

If Landscape be the best test of this quality of

On Anything

adventure in English poets and the Milton as their standard, so the mystic character of English verse appears in them and in him. No period could be so formal as to stifle or even to hide this demand of English writers for Mystery and for emotions communicable only by an art allied to music. The passion is so strong that many ill-acquainted with foreign literature will deny such literature any poetic quality because they do not find in it the unmistakable thrill which the English reader demands of a poet as he demands it of a musician. As Landscape might be taken for the best test of Adventure, so of this appetite for the Mysterious the best measurable test is rhythm. Highly accentuated rhythm and emphasis are the marks and the concomitants of that spirit. As powerful a line as any in the language for suddenly evoking intense feeling by no perceptible artifice is that line in *Lycidas*—

Smooth-sliding Mincius, crowned with vocal reeds.

I confess I can never read that line but I remember a certain river of twenty years ago, nor does revisiting that stream and seeing it again with my eyes so powerfully recall what once it was to those who loved it as does this deathless line. It seems as though the magical power of the poet escaped the effect of time in a way that the senses cannot, and a man curious in such matters might find the existence of such gifts to be a proof of human immortality. The pace at which Milton rides his verse, the strong constraint within which he binds it, deeply accentuate this power of rhythm and the mystical effect it bears. Now you would say a trumpet, now a chorus of human voices, now a flute, now a single distant song. From the fortieth to the fifty-fifth line of the third book *Paradise Lost* has all the power and nature of a solemn chant; the large complaint in it is the complaint of an organ, and one may say indeed in this connection that only one thing is lacking in all the tones Milton commanded; he disdained intensity of grief as most artists will disdain intensity of terror. But whereas intensity of terror is no fit subject for man's pen, and has appealed only to the dirtier of our little modern fellows, intense grief has been from the very beginning thought a just subject for verse.

Τῆλε δ' ἀπὸ κρατὸς χέε δέσματα σιγαλόεντα
Ἄμπυκα κεκρύφαλόν τ', ἠδὲ πλεκτὴν ἀναδέσμην
Κρήδεμνόν θ', ὅ ῥά οἱ δῶκε χρυσέη 'Αφροδίτη
Ἤματι τῷ, ὅτε μιν κορυθαίολος ἠγάγεθ' Ἕκτωρ
Ἐκ δόμου 'Ηετίωνος, ἐπεὶ πόρε μυρία ἔδνα.

Milton will have none of it. It is the absence of that note which has made so many hesitate before the glorious achievement of *Lycidas*, and in this passage which I quote, where Milton comes nearest to the cry of sorrow, it is still no more than what I have called it, a solemn chant.

. . . . Thus with the year
Seasons return ; but not to me returns
Day, or the sweet approach of Ev'n or Morn,

On Anything

Or sign of vernal bloom, or Summer's Rose,
Or flocks, or herds, or human face divine;
But cloud instead, and ever-during dark
Surrounds me, from the chearful waies of men
Cut off, and, for the Book of knowledge fair,
Presented with a Universal blanc
Of Nature's works, to mee expung'd and ras'd,
And wisdome at one entrance quite shut out.
So much the rather thou, Celestial light,
Shine inward, and the mind through all her powers
Irradiate; there plant eyes, all mist from thence
Purge and disperse, that I may see and tell
Of things invisible to mortal sight.

There is one other character in Milton wherein he
stands not so much for English Letters as for a
feature in English nature as a whole, which is a sort
of standing apart of the individual. Where this may
be good and where evil it is not for a short appreciation to discuss. It is profoundly national and nowhere will you see it more powerfully than in the
verse of this man. Of his life we all know it to be
true, but I say it appears even in his verse. There is
a sort of *noli me tangere* in it all as though he desired
but little friendship and was not broken by one
broken love, and contemplated God and the fate of
his own soul in a lonely manner; of all the things
he drew the thing he could never draw was a collec-
tivity.

HANS CHRISTIAN ANDERSEN

WHAT a great thing it is in this perplexed, confused, and, if not unhappy at least unrestful time,
to come across a thing which is cleanly itself! What
a pleasure it is amid our entwining controversies to
find straightness, and among our confused noises a
chord.   Hans Christian Andersen is a good type of
that simplicity ; and his own generation recognised
him at once ; now, when those contemporaries who
knew him best are for the most part dead, their
recognition is justified.   Of men for whom so much
and more is said by their contemporaries, how many
can stand the test which his good work now stands,
and stands with a sort of sober triumph ?   Contemporary praise has a way of gathering dross.   We all
know why.   There is the fear of this, the respect
for that ; there is the genuine unconscious attachment to a hundred unworthy and ephemeral things ;
there is the chance philosophy of the moment over-
weighing the praise-giver.   In a word, perhaps not
half-a-dozen of the great men who wrote in the
generation before our own would properly stand this
test of a neat and unfringed tradition.   It is not to

be pretended that according to that test so must men be judged. Many of the very greatest, Hugo for instance, and in his line, Huxley (a master of English); or, again, to go further back, the great Byron, would not pass the test.

Things have been said about most men, great or little, in our fevered time, so exaggerated, so local and so lacking balance, whether of experience or of the fear of posterity, that contemporary opinion should not be allowed by its misfortunes to weigh them down. But a man has a quality of his own when he is so made that even his contemporaries do him justice, and that was the case with Hans Christian Andersen. I will bargain that if our letters survive five hundred years, this excellent writer will quietly survive. Even the French may incorporate him. And next it is the business of one who praises so much to ask in what the excellence of this writer consists. It is threefold: in the first place, he always said what he thought; in the second place, he was full of all sorts of ways of saying it; and, in the third place, he said only what he had to say.

To say what one thinks, that is, to tell the truth, is so exceedingly rare that one may almost call it a grace in a man. Just those same manifold strings which pull contemporary criticism hither and thither, and which have made me suggest above that contemporary criticism commonly belittles a man in the long run, just those same strings pull at every writer to make him conform to what he knows to be false

Hans Christian Andersen

in his time. But some men—with limitations, it is true, and only by choosing a particular framework— manage to tell the truth all their lives ; those men, if they have other literary qualities, are secure of the future.

And this leads me to the second point, which is that Andersen could not only tell the truth but tell it in twenty different ways, and of a hundred different things. Now this character has been much exaggerated among literary men in importance, because literary men, perceiving it to be the differentiation which marks out the great writer from the little, think it to be the main criterion of letters. It is not the main criterion ; but it is a permanent necessity in great writing. There is no great writing without this multiplicity, which is sometimes called imagination, sometimes experience, and sometimes judgment, but which is in its essence a proper survey of the innumerable world. This quality it is which makes the great writers create what are called " characters " ; and whether we recognise those " characters " as portraits drawn from the real world (they are such in Balzac), or as figments (they are such in Dickens), or as heroines and heroes (they are such in Shakespeare and in Homer, if you will excuse me), yet that they exist and live in the pages of the writer means that he had in him that quality of contemplation which corresponds in our limited human nature to the creative power.

Lastly, I say that Andersen said what he had to

say and no more. This quality in writers is not restraint—a futile word dear to those who cannot write—it is rather a sort of chastity in the pen. The writer of this kind is one who unconsciously does not add; if any one were to ask him why he should not add an ornament or anything supposititious, he would be bewildered and perhaps might answer: "Why should I?" The instinct behind it is that which produces all terseness, all exactitude, and all economy in style.

Andersen, then, had all those three things which make a great writer, and a very great writer he is.

Note that he chose his framework, or, at any rate, that he was persuaded to it. He could not have been so complete had he not addressed himself to children, and it is his glory that he is read in childhood. There is no child but can read Hans Christian Andersen, and I at least have come across no man who, having read him in childhood, does not continue to read him throughout life. He wrote nothing that was not for the enlivening or the sustenance or the guiding of the human soul; he wrote nothing that suggested questions only. If one may speak of him in terms a trifle antiquated (or rather for the moment old-fashioned), he was instinct with charity, and therefore he is still full of life.

Having said so much of Andersen in general, something should be said of him in particular. He was Northern; you always feel as you read him that if his scene is laid in the open air, the air is fresh and often frosty ; that if he is talking indoors the room is cosy and often old. Certain passions which the North lacks are lacking in him, both upon their good and upon their evil side. He is never soldierly, and he is never revengeful ; he is never acute with the desire for life, but, again, he is never envious. Those who read him and who are also Northern may well be in love with Denmark. It is a triumph of our civilisation that this little land, quite outside the limits of the Roman Empire, not riven by any of the Empires' great vital resurrections, undisturbed by the vision of the Twelfth and of the Thirteenth Centuries, spared from the march of Napoleon's armies, should be so completely European. What could be more European to-day than that well-organised, contented, peasant State ? It is a good irony to put against the blundering prophecies of barbaric people that beyond the Germanies this secure and happy State exists. One might put it in a phrase a little too epigrammatic and say that as one reads Hans Christian Andersen one remembers Elsinore, and one recalls the good architecture of Copenhagen. If ever any misfortune again shall threaten that State, and if barbarism attempts to play the fool with it, something that really is the conscience of Europe and not the empty and sham organisation to which that phrase is too often prostituted will arise and protect the Danes.

THE CHRISTMAS OF 1808

No British Army in force has capitulated in Europe for many generations. It is the peculiar historical position of this country. That historical fact lends to the common history of the schools and universities an attitude towards military history in general which is commonly distorted, but it lends to the policy of the country as a whole a confident tradition, the strength and value of which it is impossible to exaggerate.

The nearest touch to such a disaster, if we except the sieges, was passed during the days in which these words are written and read; the close thing came about in the days just before and just after Christmas, one hundred and two years ago. I will attempt to describe as simply as I can the nature of that adventure.

It must first of all be premised that, in the words of Napier, position determines the fate of armies. No truth is more apparent to the soldier, none more forgotten by the civilian—and more especially by the civilian touched with the unmilitary vice of Jingoism. Position determines the fate of armies,

154

and, armaments being supposedly equal, he is a great or a fortunate general who, in the critical moment, has so arranged matters that disposition is upon his side, or who by some stroke of luck is in that advantage. There are exceptions to this truth. Certain decisive battles (though very few) have utterly determined campaigns; and among these battles some, again, have been won at a drive, and by a sort of impetus, the factor of position being so simple as to be negligible, or so equally balanced as to advantage neither side and be eliminated. But, as a rule, it is true even of decisive actions, that position is the determining factor. It is necessarily true of the strategy of a campaign, and it is with this consideration that I return to the particular crisis of the British Army at the close of December 1808.

Sir John Moore, as every one knows, had raided right into the North of Spain, with the object of withdrawing the pressure of the French upon the South of that country. It was in the South that French ambition had found its first check, and that Napoleon's plan had been warped by the unexpected and, as it were, impossible capitulation of Baylen. Close upon twenty thousand of the French forces had there laid down their arms. The Emperor came in person to restore the fortunes of his house; it was in the South that resistance could best be expected; by the occupation of the South that he might put himself at ease over the whole territory, and from the South that the English operations were destined to draw him.

On the 21st of December, a Wednesday, Lord Paget, with the Tenth and Fifteenth Hussars, surprised an advanced body of French Cavalry at Sahagun. It was the extreme limit of Moore's great raid; the town was occupied, and all the Thursday, all the Friday, Moore halted there with his force of some twenty-three thousand and sixty guns. He was nearly two hundred miles from the port on the sea-coast, whereto he must retire if he would escape. In front of him was Soult, against whom it was his business, if he were undisturbed, to march from Sahagun immediately; but upon his right, nearly as far off as the sea, though not quite so far, a matter of a hundred and fifty to a hundred and seventy miles, Napoleon, at Madrid, commanded the best and the largest of the armies in Spain. Sixty thousand men, with a hundred and fifty guns, lay at the gates of Madrid, and during those same hours in which the British Army had marched into Sahagun, Napoleon's great force began to move northward over the Guadarrama.

I will not here describe that famous march: I have done so elsewhere at greater length: but the reader, to appreciate the conditions of this great duel, must imagine a country denuded and largely mountainous, deep in snow, and subject throughout those days to intolerable weather; and the race upon the issue of which depended so many and such final things was run at a time and in a place when one would have thought that no man could be abroad. But the protagonists of the Revolutionary wars were not men like ourselves.

Christmas Day fell upon the Sunday. Moore had got ahead of his supplies; they had reached him on the Friday, and on the Saturday, Christmas Eve, he had intended to go forward and attack the opponent before him. But on that same Friday when, in the night, his Infantry were already beginning to march eastward, he heard of Napoleon's amazing feat; he knew that he had succeeded in drawing the great commander northward, but he knew also, since that commander could work miracles, that the distance separating them would be crossed with a swiftness not to be measured by the old rules of war, and that the vast force three times his own would, if he hesitated, be found holding the snow-blocked roads between his position and the sea. The order to advance was cancelled, the order to retreat was given. By Christmas Eve Baird and Hope were on the line of the Esla River; on Christmas Day, Sunday, the troops were passing that obstacle. On Monday, the 26th, the baggage and the last of the army, under Moore's own eye, were crossing by the bridge of Castro Gonzalo before Benevente, and the trick was done. There was a thick fog, the passage was far slower than the strained intelligence of the imperilled commander had designed. On that same day, the 26th, Napoleon was at Tordesillas, one long day's march away from the Esla River. He had covered in that dash of three days and a half a hundred and twenty miles, but he was too late. He was too late by half a day.

In the dark and storm-driven night of that Monday the extreme van of Napoleon's horse rode up to the bridge of Castro Gonzalo. They were unsupported, of course, and rode far before the army to discover; but, though it was not contact in any serious sense, there is something very worthily dramatic in the appearance of those tall horsemen suddenly in the night through the blinding snow, come up just too late to do more than watch the escape of Moore's column.

By the next day the purpose of the British commander was achieved : Napoleon knew he could no longer intercept : the bridge was destroyed. The opportunity of recording the envelopment and destruction of a British force was lost to Napoleon ; he abandoned to Soult the further long pursuit, which is called in history the retreat upon Corunna.

ON COMMUNICATIONS

THERE is nothing more curious in the material change which is passing so rapidly over the modern world than what I may call the Romance of Communication.

With the Romance of Discovery every one is thoroughly acquainted. The modern world is saturated with that form of romance; it has permeated all our literature and is still the theme of most of our books of travel. But like all things which have attained a literary position, the Romance of Discovery already belongs to the past. Not that nothing remains to be discovered: on the contrary, the modern world has hardly yet begun to appreciate how it may penetrate from detail to detail and find perpetually something new in that which it thinks it knows, but the great broad unknown spaces, the horizons quite new to Europeans which break upon them for the first time, are now no longer left to the explorer. With the romance of communication, luckily for us, there is another, a newer and, in a certain sense, a much wider field. Many who have travelled largely have felt this, but it has not yet, I think, been expressed.

On Anything

What I mean by the Romance of Communication is this: that the establishment of regular lines for ocean traffic, the building of railways and, above all, of good roads, have made it possible for a multitude of men to see those contrasts which travel can afford, and this development of modern travel has just begun to afford our generation, and will afford with much greater generosity the generation to come, an opportunity for feeling physically the complexity and variety and wonder of the world. This is a good thing.

Not so long ago it was a difficult matter for a man to go from some Northern part of Europe, such as England, to so isolated a community as that which inhabits the Island of Majorca. Now it is easy for a man and costs him but a few pounds to go from England to Barcelona, and from Barcelona he can sail with a rapid and regular service to the port of Palma. When he reaches that port he cannot but feel the Romance, finding this little isolated State wealthy and contented in the midst of the sea. Corsica, of which men know so little, is similarly at hand to-day, and so are the Valleys of the Pyrenees, especially of the Spanish valleys upon which as yet there is hardly any Northern literature or experience. In a year or two we shall have the railway through the Cerdagne, and another line will take one up the Valley of the Ariège into the middle part of Northern Spain.

But of all these benefits to the mind which the

modern charge is procuring, I know of none more remarkable than the entry into the Desert.

That portion of Northern Africa which the French have reclaimed for Europe, and which was throughout the existence of the Roman Empire an integral part of European civilisation, consists of the great table-land buttressed to the north and the south by mountain ranges, and crossed in its middle part by parallel outcrops of high rock. This plateau stretches for somewhat more than a thousand miles all along the southern shore of the Western Mediterranean. If the reader will take a map he will see jutting out from the general contour of Africa, an oblong as it were, the eastern end of which is Tunis, the western end Morocco. All that oblong is the tableland of which I speak. The coast is warm, fertile, densely cultivated and populous; full of ports and cities and the coming and going of ships. The highlands behind and to the south of the coast line are more arid, very cold in winter, baking in summer, and always dry and rugged to our Northern eyes. But they are habitable, the population is spreading upon them, and they contain the past relics of the old Roman civilisation which prove what man can do with them when their water supply is stored and their soil is cultivated.

Now this habitable land suddenly ceases, and falls into the Desert of Sahara. The demarkation is abrupt and is everywhere noticeable to the eye. It is indeed more noticeable in the eastern than in the

On Anything

western part. The limit between what Miss Bell has called, in a fine book of hers, "the Desert and the Sown," is more than a day's march in width upon the Moroccan frontier; indeed it is several days' march, and one is not over-sure when one has left the habitable soil and when one has reached the inhospitable sand at the eastern end. The limits are not only marked sharply by a differentiation in the climate and the vegetation, but also by an abrupt escarpment. The Atlas (as the plateau of Northern Africa is generally called) falls in huge, precipitous red cliffs right down upon the Sahara. It so happens that these cliffs, just at the point where they are most abrupt and most rugged, and most romantic, are cleft by a profound gorge through which the Wady Biskra runs very clear and cold, filled with the melting of the snow upon the high mountain of Aures to the north of it. This gap in the cliffs the Romans knew well. They had a military station here to guard them against the ravages of the nomad tribes who afterwards, in the form of the Arabian Invasion, overran their African province and turned it from an European and a Christian to an Asiatic and Mohammedan thing. The Romans called that gorge "The Kick of Hercules," as though the god had here by a stroke of his foot broken away from the cultivated north toward the Desert. Through this gap ran their military road, and here, as a formation of the gorge demanded, they carried that road over the river, the

On Communications

Wady Biskra, upon the bridge the stones of which still remain, though renovated and supported by modern work, to recall the greatness of the empire.

The Arabs, in their turn, have called this astonishing breach " Foum es Sahara "--the mouth of the Sahara ; and, as is always the case where they found a Roman bridge, they have added the name El Kantara, the bridge. For it is remarkable that the Arabs were unable to continue Roman work, especially in masonry, save where they had a large Roman population to help them after their conquest, and the bridges which the Romans had built were regarded by them with a sort of superstitious reverence.

Now this Mouth of the Sahara, this gap in the glaring wall of the Desert, has, by a coincidence which has its obvious geographical cause, and which is to be discovered in many another pass throughout Europe and Northern Africa, served for modern methods of communication the purpose which it served for the ancients. It is the nearest approach which the Desert makes to the sea-coast ; it is the approach involving the least engineering effort, the most obvious and the most natural entry from the northern cultivated land on to the waterless sandy waste. Therefore, modern civilisation has used it, and you get here more than anywhere else that romance of sudden contrast with which, as I have said, modern methods of travel have gifted the modern world. The French first built down this track a military road, as hard, excellent and well graded as any that you will find in Europe. It not only goes through the gorge, but right on into the sand of the desert, bounded upon either side by masonry, and it has reached, or very soon will reach, Biskra without a break.

Some time after this road had been planned, a railway was constructed along the same track, with certain divergences where the gradient of the highway was too steep for the rails and where therefore long curves were necessary. Whether a man goes by the road or the rail, this is what he sees—and he had best see it in early spring, or what is with us in England late winter. As the road and the rail wind downwards from the little plateaux, by great steps as it were from one level to another, the traveller has about him such scenery as has accompanied him for the last hundred miles: fields of cotton, the trees proper to a temperate climate, and rugged, rocky ridges cropping up from the cultivated soil. There is nothing around him to remind him of what is called "The East," except the camel preceding its master up or down the great highway and the distinctive dress of the natives; for the climate, the crops, and the temperature, the quality of the sunlight, he might be on one of the plains of Western America, which indeed this part of Africa most nearly resembles.

He comes to a clean little inn entirely French in architecture, surrounded by a cool and quiet garden,

and with the river running behind it. He walks on
a few hundred yards through the gorge, and quite
suddenly at the turning of a corner the Desert and
all its horizon breaks upon his eyes. He sees a
waste of hot, red, unusable sand, a brilliant oasis of
palm trees, and even the sun, small and glaring
above that plain, seems something different from
the familiar light which he had received but an hour
before.

It is the most complete contrast, the most sudden
and memorable revelation which modern travel
affords. And if I had to advise any one who with
short leisure desired some experience of modern
travel, at least in the way of landscape, I would
advise him to visit this astounding place. It has
already found its way into many English books, but
the great mass of people who could enjoy it do not
yet know how exceedingly easy is its access. For
travellers even to so near a place like to put on an
air of mystery. There is no one with a fortnight to
spare and £20 to spend who cannot walk or bicycle
or motor to this place at the right time of the year
(for in summer the heat is insupportable and in
winter the snow on the high northern plains makes
travel difficult). Any one who will take that journey
would have a memory to last him all his life.

There are those who say that the popularisation of
wonderful things is the spoiling of them. I have
never been able to agree. Places are not spoiled by
the multitude of those who reach them, but by the

character of those who reach them, and no one will journey to this meeting place of the East and the West, I think, save with a desire to wonder and to observe, which of itself breeds reverence. Such men may come in any numbers and the place will be the better for them. At any rate, I repeat, it ought to be known to any one who has the sum or the time to spare, that a revelation of such a kind is quite close at hand, for as yet hundreds of Englishmen with far more than that leisure and infinitely more than that wealth are ignorant of the place and its opportunities; and your quickest way is by Marseilles and Bona, and on your way I beseech you to stop and see Timgad, which is a dead Roman city lying silent and empty under the sun upon the Edge of the Desert.

ASTARTE

IF you stand outside the old fortifications of the town of Toul and look eastward toward the German peoples, you see a long even line of hills, very high but not quite mountainous; they end in a sharp dip, and rise again, and terminate in an isolated summit which, like so many of the striking conical peaks of Europe, is dedicated to St. Michael.

These heights, like all the crests which surround the basin of that entrenched camp, are fortified, both with complete works and with connecting trenches and batteries; save in the gap between the isolated hill and the ridge I have mentioned the guns are everywhere. In this gap, in the hollow of it and upon the hillside, is a little village which, like all the villages on the actual line of the encircling forts, is wholly dominated by the soldiery; these furnish it with all its trade, these give it its few adventures and its manner of life. The peasants are woken summer and winter by the sound of bugles; the heavy firing of practice is a usual thing to them; a profitable commerce with a garrison twice as numerous as the civil population enriches those who work upon their land.

On Anything

In this village there lived one of those families which are poor in a country of free men through their own fault; they had land, of course; no rent was asked of them; they were in a community which had now for many ages administered itself, and had for more than a hundred years forgotten the oppression of a territorial class. Nevertheless, by some vice of temperament, they lived like slatterns, and if they cultivated at all some tiny patch of their ruined and weedy holding, it was but just so much as would keep their souls within their bodies, and they preferred chance begging and barefoot jobs at the railway-station or in the streets of the town. Their house was more a cave than a hut; it was dug out of the hillside, with beaten earth walls, save where the front portion of it jutted out, and was roofed with old bits of corrugated iron borrowed or stolen from the sappers. These were supported by a jumble of ramshackle wood, old railway-sleepers, and here and there were gaps stopped roughly with canvas.

In such a place, surrounded by brothers and sisters of all ages, and the only houseworker to a drunken and worthless mother, lived, by accident, one of those women who have such great power in this world. Her ugliness was singular; it had nothing to do with that power save perhaps to enhance it. Her hair, which was sparse and crisp, was of a bright, unpleasing red, harsh and offensive; her eyes were green and stood very far apart in her head;

168

her mouth was large and very decided and firm. It is not by any recapitulation of her features (though any one who had once seen them would always remember them) that one can give the impression of her power. This rather proceeded from a gesture, a manner, and a whole being which was the continual outer manifestation of a certain kind of soul. There was strength in all her gestures, an upstanding challenge in the poise of her body whether she worked or walked, and a sort of creative handling of things whenever she grasped them which at once arrested the attention of a man. Her excessive poverty and the gross carelessness of her surroundings, by contrast greatly enhanced these things.

The young soldiers cared very little for mysteries; their religion was indifferent to them, their knowledge of the perils and of the adventures of the soul was less than that of children; for those who might have guessed at the mysterious things which everywhere surround our existence, even at twenty-one, had such imaginings drowned and purged out of them by continual labour in the open air, by hours of grooming and of riding, by the deep and glorious fatigue of such a life, by sleep in the night, by hunger and by fellowship. Nevertheless, among the more leisured, that is, among the non-commissioned officers, there was one man who fell under the spell. He was handsome, unintelligent, lacking in judgment, and perhaps twenty-five years of age. His father was a large farmer to the north of Rheims;

he had a very fair allowance from home; he was regular and did his service well; he was, so far as the non-commissioned ranks can be in any army, popular with the men. This fellow felt the spell. He felt it neither deeply nor violently, for his nature was one on which the great emotions could have no play; but he would seek such duties as brought him to the village, he would intrigue to be sent upon any inspection of the reserve forces or with provisions up into the forts, or upon any other business which would give him for a few moments a chance of seeing her at the door of that miserable hovel, and of exchanging half-a-dozen words from the saddle. His leave he would often spend in the inn of that village, some said in her company (but I doubt if this were true); he would have taken her once into Nancy to see some public show or other, but she would not go.

Between the end of winter and the start for camp, the thing had become as much a habit to him as his own name, and by a sort of code which the regiment observed, his habit was respected and passed by; indeed, to have become so immeshed regarded no one but himself, and the singular net that had been thrown over him was not one which others envied. But there was one who envied him.

When he had been Vaguemestre, that is, the sergeant deputed to fetch the letters of the regiment, and often also when he had gone out to note the condition of the reserve horses or upon any other message, he had taken with him one of the two-year men, a Belgian who had crossed the frontier to find work in his teens, and was not ill content to have been caught by the conscription, for he was utterly destitute and knew neither father nor mother. This man was dark, short and broad ; he was kindly in temper and, one would have said, an animal for stupidity. He was possessed of great physical strength ; he was a faithful servant and follower where he was employed. And his Sergeant who thus favoured him would often see to it that his service should be lightened in one way or another, and made his life more easy to him than it was to the other drivers of the battery. He was popular, every one helped him, he had done harm to no one, he was always willing. He very rarely spoke, amid all that voluble clatter of young men, and when he did, it was to crack some simple peasant joke or to repeat some old tag of a proverb.

But one day the head of the room who happened to have no stripes and was no more than an older soldier, or, as it was called in that service, "an ancient," found him sitting on his bed and crying. The lout was crying in a gentle but despairing sort of way. The ancient was a rough man, a miner and rather brutal. He would have none of it. And just as he was making things rough for the Belgian, the Sergeant's voice came down the wooden corridors calling him to saddle the two beasts : and all the Belgian did was to refuse. It was a quite unheard-of

thing. There was no elasticity in the service; and if
any one in authority said "Do this," to say "I will
not," or even to be slow in obedience, was as grave,
or rather as unknown, as is a crime of violence
among wealthy men.

Now the Sergeant, with more womanliness and
discernment than one would have thought any one
could have shown in such a place, made no noise
about it, but came in to see what miracle had happened. He saw the lad sitting there upon his bed
with his coarse face full of despair, and he did not
in the least understand what could have happened.
The eyes of the lad were as full of wonder and of
terror and of hopelessness as though he had seen
some full tragedy of human life. The Sergeant
shrugged his shoulders and let him be, and to save
his being worried sent him off upon an easy job until
he should come round. Then taking another man to
saddle the two horses and to accompany him, he
went off upon his usual round towards the hills, upon
some official errand or other which he had managed
to secure. But when he got there he found in the
village, without leave, and having run and panted
through the newly ploughed fields, this Belgian
fellow, looking like an angry dog, sullen, and with
new tears in his eyes, standing outside the door of
the hovel.

He ordered him back; he rode his horse after him
as the Belgian obeyed, and began trudging suddenly
away, and said that he would not report it, but that

it was a piece of madness, and that if that sort of thing went on it ended in Africa.

The Belgian said nothing, but plodded off, his enormous strength apparent in every step; and apparent also in the set of his neck and shoulders, and the bending of his head, something of doom. When he got back to quarters he got a ball cartridge from the workroom—no one knows how—he put it in one of the gunner's carbines, which he took from the rack—he had never handled such a weapon before—pulled off the boot from his sockless right foot, put the barrel of the thing in his mouth, and with his toe pressed down the trigger. In this way he killed himself.

I have told the thing exactly as it happened. Then many of the young men first knew that our lives are not wholly of our own ordering, or, to put it better, learned that to ride one's destiny needs in the soul of a man a training, a quickness and a constancy like that which, in the body, helps a man to ride a strong horse and to control him.

THE HUNGRY STUDENT

It was with great astonishment combined with a
sense of misfortune that I discovered the other day
in a garret off the King's road in Chelsea a poor hack
formerly of my acquaintance, who in his endeavour
to keep body and soul together had formerly been
distinguished or rather ridiculous among journalists
by his excursions into every conceivable subject and
his preparedness to write any sort of books that a
publisher might order of him.

When I found him after these many years he was
lying in the last stages of some disease the name of
which I forget but which anyhow was mortal; and
it was the character in the disease which most
affected him—to its scientific appellation he was
indifferent.

He confessed to me that he had long had it on his
conscience that in a work of his now long forgotten
he had promised the reader to tell a certain story,
and that this promise had never been fulfilled.

" It is in the beginning of the book," he whispered
feebly as his dying eyes were turned towards the
four chimneys of the electrical works, " that I prom-

ised to tell the story—nay, two stories ; I promised to tell the story of The Hungry Student, and also the story of the Brigand of Radicofani. Both these stories weigh heavily upon my conscience. I have promised," he continued in a nervous manner which was tragically affecting, "and I have not redeemed my promise. Readers of mine may have died, still wondering what the truth may be. I beg you, therefore, to take this manuscript" (and he motioned with his wasted hand to some sheets of paper by the side of his bed) "and to give it to the world. At once," he said with the haste and fever of a dying man, "to-morrow you shall come and I will give you the second manuscript concerning the Brigand of Radicofani." ("Both," he moaned, "I took from the writings of others.") "And then I can die in peace."

I took the manuscript and left him, and to fulfil his last wishes I publish it here.

. . . . . .

A student in the University of Paris had the misfortune to be wholly deprived of money in any form, and such credit as he had once enjoyed was also entirely exhausted. It was now thirty-six hours since he had eaten any memorable meal, and during that long period of time he had tasted no more than one roasted potato, a pennyworth of chestnuts, a cup of coffee, and a little bread which he had kept in his pocket from the day before yesterday, and which was therefore of a hard and ungracious sort. Even that had been consumed in the small hours of the morning,

On Anything

and he sat upon a stone bench in the evening of the day about fifty yards from the Odéon Theatre, carefully considering what course he should pursue, and determining, if it were necessary, to thieve ; for hunger had got him where hunger gets us all—which is not, as too many assert, in the stomach, but in the throat and palate and brain.

As he there sat he thought of delicious things ; not of a mere filling, but of rare matters. He had longings. He remembered that beans, green beans, are better crisp than soft ; and he thought of irrecoverable aubergines, and of what an onion was when it was well fried, and of larded chickens, and of great Touranian pears, and of the kind of wine called Chinon ; he thought of all these things. But there is this quality about hunger, that the imagination does not satisfy it in any degree at all, but stimulates it only, and he was tortured as he sat upon that bench. Remember that he had not any money at all. He even recalled as he there sat the excellent taste of fresh bread and chocolate, and he was about to get up and walk off the memory of such things when a confused and growing rumour coming up the steep street round the corner broke upon him. It was the noise of many young men. It was almost military in its character, though it had no precision, for one felt in it the advance of numbers. It swelled with every moment, and at last there swung round the corner and up towards his bench a considerable body of students who were walking rapidly, excitedly,

176

and happily, gesticulating freely and telling each other good news, while a very powerful and loud-voiced young man led them on. He could hear snatches of what was said by this company. One was crying : " It is surely the best cooking in the world ! " Another, " I care nothing for the cooking, but what wine ! " Two others were eagerly disputing whether the lark or the thrush were the better bird, and one was hoping that there would be a chaudfroid of nightingales. Some few sang songs, others in a sort of contented silence went forward eagerly ; all evidently had before them some great goal.

As the Herd swept by him a lean young man with black hair just stooped in passing the Hungry Student and whispered : " Would you like to eat to-night ? " He whispered back " Yes." " Then," said the first, whose eyes burned like coals, " up you get and follow, and hold your tongue until you learn the tricks of the rest."

So the Hungry Student rose up at once and went forward, mingling with the rest ; and still their robust leader plunged through the streets before them like a captain bringing on a young army of saviours into an oppressed land. Now and then this captain would turn round and walk backward like a bandmaster or a drum major, shouting out good news of food to come and of the wine that has been pressed in Paradise.

So they went until they came to the Boulevard,

which they crossed, one of them fighting with a policeman on the way. The band plunged into the narrower streets, and came at last to a little open square where was a restaurant with a balcony upon the first floor, and upon that balcony an awning. The name written above the restaurant was this: "The Widow Bertrand—a house founded in 1837." They all trooped in.

Upon the balcony a table was spread ; there were other tables in the room with which the balcony communicated. At these some few and rather diffident guests had sat down ; but the large table was reserved for the Herd. They took their places noisily, and falling upon a few little sardines and one or two stale strips of sausage they began loudly exclaiming upon every side at the excellence of the fare.

The Hungry Student said nothing, though he wondered much, but seizing an enormous piece of bread he ate it all up with the rapidity of a storm, and heard round him as he did so ceaseless exclamations of enthusiastic surprise. The wine was very thin and sour—but the wine of students is always so. What astonished him was to see a curly-headed fellow, very Northern in type, suddenly jump up and shout, so that all the street below could hear—

"Upon my word this is amazing ! Send for Gaston !"

Gaston, a very weary waiter, came.

"Gaston," said the Northerner, " I really must know where the Widow gets this wine ! "

The Hungry Student

The whole chorus of them shouted together: " Yes, Gaston, you must tell us where she gets this wine !"

Gaston murmured something which the Hungry Student did not hear.

"Oh, do not be afraid," shouted the Northerner, "we will not give the secret away. But what wine !" he added, turning round to his companions, who applauded with their hands. " We will get it through the Widow. She shall provide it to us. A wine like this is not to be missed." And he took the miserable stuff and sipped it slowly from his glass, cocking one eye up wisely towards the ceiling like a knowing fellow.

There followed bad soup, bad fish, bad meat, bad vegetables, and bad roast. But the Hungry Student was not particular, and he fed. Lord ! how heartily he fed ! He fed so heartily that he got into that mood when a man thinks he will never be hungry again. He ate great quantities of cheese, which alone of all the courses was served them with some liberality. He drank their coffee, and the whole host rose to go. He was still in a profound mystery.

An elderly woman, whose face betrayed keen avarice overspread with conventional courtesy, bade them good-night as they left her establishment. They cheered her, and the leader of the band kissed her warmly upon both cheeks. Then they went out, turned into the Rue Cujas, and quite suddenly their enthusiasm wholly disappeared, and a council of war

On Anything

was summoned. The powerful man, the leader, stood in their midst, gave the recommendation and took counsel with his peers.

" It is the last time ! " he said grimly.

" Do you mean," said the dark-haired student who had first whispered to the Hungry Student as he passed, before the meal, " do you mean the Widow will not receive us again ? "

" You are right," said the leader, in a solemn tone. " The bargain was for five nights ; she has extended it to six. But it seems "—bitterly—" that we have done our work too well. There is no need of a seventh. Only yesterday the business was bought by a very foolish fellow from Auxerre."

" That," said a short fat young man, who had not yet spoken, " accounts for the intolerable wine."

The leader shrugged his shoulders, and said gloomily : " Friend, it was the same old wine, but from the bottom of the barrel."

" Then there is no meal for to-morrow," said a fourth man, anxiously, a red-headed, vague-eyed man who had gone in for Anarchism the year before, but was at that particular moment a Symbolist.

" Well," said the leader, " there is a meal for to-morrow. But the conditions are a little hard."

" Where is it to be ? What is the rendezvous ? What are those conditions ? " cried several voices.

The strong leader obtained silence, and said : " I can tell you at once ; Berteaux wants to sell his

180

place by private treaty next week, and he will take us from to-morrow."

" For how many days ? " broke in a silent man who had not yet spoken.

" A full week," said the leader.

" Well, that's good enough," said the dark man sullenly.

" Yes, but the point is," said the leader, " there is another offer : the new railway station wants to start a meal at a fixed price."

" It will be better cooking," said the red-haired Symbolist doubtfully.

" You are right," answered the leader, a little wearily, " but it is one of their conditions that one should eat at the absurd hour of half-past five, and hurry through the meal exclaiming all the while chance things about the express to Toulouse, and noting the rapidity of the service."

" I will never do that ! " said the red-headed man firmly, amid murmurs of approval. " If I must eat their deathly stuff I will eat it, but I will not be hurried into the bargain ; and half-past five is the hour for poisons, not for food. Absinthe is mine."

" No, Berteaux is the man," said the leader with a sigh. He put it to the vote, as is the fashion with the French. There was a large majority for Berteaux.

Next day that same enthusiastic whirl of youth went through other streets of the learned centre of Europe, their lips vivacious, their eyes aflame, to

On Anything

give Berteaux's business a selling value, and themselves to have food for nothing.

In this way was the Hungry Student filled.

.   .   .   .   .   .

Next day, having sent in this manuscript that you have read, I called upon my poor friend to receive the Brigand of Radicofani; but you may imagine how shocked I was to hear that he was dead.

182

THE BRIGAND OF RADICOFANI

It is with the utmost pleasure that I am able to communicate to the English-speaking world a literary document of capital importance which my readers had only too great reason to mourn as lost. It will be remembered that my poor friend the Hack, recently deceased in the neighbourhood of the King's road, suffered in his last hours from the fear that the world might never receive his two masterpieces which he had so long promised them, "The Story of the Hungry Student" and "The Brigand of Radicofani." It will also be remembered that on reaching his humble lodgings after the publication of the first, I discovered him to be dead, and feared, therefore, that the second of these two classics would never be discovered. I am delighted to say that a Rag and Bottle Merchant and Dealer in Kitchen Stuff near The World's End (which is a landmark in that neighbourhood) has been found in possession of the precious paper, which by a providential accident is still legible, although it had been used to wrap up two boot-brushes and a second-hand

183

pot of blacking. Such coincidences are not unknown in the history of English Letters.

·   ·   ·   ·   ·   ·

A young Colonial journalist, full of a great determination to succeed in life, but insufficiently equipped for that ambition, had occasion to visit the country north of Rome in the year 1903.   He had been sent by his proprietors to gather information upon the customs of the peasantry for a series of articles which they designed to publish; he had orders to photograph these natives with or without their leave, and to acquire such a knowledge of the local dialects as would permit him to converse with them.

With his numerous adventures in the extinct volcanoes of that district I need not detain you, nor tell you of how he was imprisoned in Ronciglione, fined by a magistrate in Viterbo, nor how he was soundly beaten by a drunken mason in the town of Bolsena, whose lovely lake he still remembers with associated feelings of admiration and regret.   It is more to my purpose to retail how in each of these towns as he wandered northwards, and at every intervening house of call, he was perpetually reminded of the Brigand of Radicofani. Some, when he would ask them questions upon their local habits, would reply, "Oh, go and discuss it with the Brigand of Radicofani"; others, when he attempted to stammer his experiences of the road, would tell him that the Brigand would make a better audience than they. The magistrate who fined him at Viterbo

The Brigand of Radicofani

made an allusion to the Brigand of Radicofani which he caught but ill, but which provoked, to his annoyance, considerable laughter in court. The policeman who locked him up in Ronciglione turned the key with an allusion to the same individual, and even the drunken mason in the very act of beating him in Bolsena bade him begone to the Brigand of Radicofani. As for Aquapendente, the town was full of rumours about this strange man, the children in the streets, who should have known better, took the young Colonial twice for the Brigand and followed him in chorus, calling him by that name; while a little brown man who was pushing a barrow assured him with great solemnity that he was taking its contents of private refreshment for the Brigand of Radicofani.

It may be imagined with what eagerness the journalist left the town next morning by the northern road and with what curiosity of attention he marked the little town of Radicofani perched upon its distant conical hill and glaring white under the hot morning. "There," said he to himself, as he laboriously panted up the last slope, "I shall find a character indeed worthy of so many pains, and discover something perhaps of permanent value for the history of this ancient land."

He seated himself in the principal room of the first inn he came to within the gate and boldly asked whether it were possible at that hour to interview the Brigand. The young woman who was the

mistress of the house looked at him for a moment
in a sort of stupor, then bursting into wild cries not
unmixed with laughter, she fled from him and left
him for quite a quarter of an hour alone ; she
returned with a little crowd of Radicofanian bur-
gesses who stood round, hats in hand, looking at
him lugubriously. At last the oldest of them, a
man with a noble head, handsome and grey, said to
him solemnly—

" Do we understand, Excellence, that you desire
to see the well-known Brigand of Radicofani ? "

" That is so," replied the journalist manfully. " I
am indeed sorry if my pursuit of such an audience
seems impertinent, for I recognise the high position
held by this gentleman in your community ; and I
am equally sorry if I have given you any trouble by
my request. But as I am deputed by a foreign
newspaper of high standing to discover what I can
of the customs of an ancient land, I could hardly
proceed onward to the notable town of Sienna and
leave behind me uninterviewed the principal
personage of your countryside."

" Not a word," said the grave leader of that band,
" it is a pleasure to serve one who takes so flattering
an interest in our poor affairs. If your Excellency
will but wait a moment and read the local newspapers, one of which he will discover to be religious,
the other of contrary tone, the Brigand shall shortly
be introduced to you."

Heartened by this promise, the young journalist

The Brigand of Radicofani

read with some care the leading articles of the greasy rags before him, and maintained his dignity and his apparent attention to the text in spite of occasional openings of the door accompanied by the giggling and elbowing of the curious who, in out-of-the-way places, infest a stranger.

At last the door opened wide before the sweeping gesture and the advancing stride of one accustomed to command, and the Brigand of Radicofani stood before the traveller.

His dress was picturesque in the extreme : he had on knee breeches ornamented with parti-coloured ribbons, his calves were swathed round with criss-cross bands, a rustic pipe hung from his belt, which also sheathed four knives of different dimensions with variegated and curious carved handles. Aslant across these he wore a naked dagger quite eighteen inches long ; a gloomy cloak depended from one shoulder ; upon his head was a steeple-crowned hat, very tall and pointed, and adorned, like the rest of his person, with ribbons of gay hue. In either ear he wore an enormous ring of gold, and black ringlets which shone with some oily substance depended in profusion from either side of his head. This extra-ordinary figure was completed by a gigantic blunder-buss with a bore about the size of a duck gun and ending in a huge bell mouth quite nine inches across.

The Brigand (for it was he) startled the journalist by asking in a terrible voice what he wanted with him, and bidding him be brief and to the point in his interrogations or demands. As he so spoke he tapped with his left hand the curious handle of his dagger, keeping his fist clenched upon his haunch and his right arm akimbo, while his left leg and foot were advanced in a martial and even in a threatening manner. The young Colonial, who was acquainted—by his reading—with many situations of danger, summoned all his firmness, begged the Brigand to share the wine which stood before him, and assured him that he had only disturbed his leisure in order to hear from the lips of one so justly prominent in the ancient and noble town of Radicofani memories of its great past intermingled, as he hoped, with records of the Brigand's individual career.

Mollified by such an address, the great man sank into the rickety chair opposite the journalist, assumed the attitude of the warrior at ease, and began with plentiful and dramatic gesture the recital of many things.

Brigandage, he assured his companion, was now by no means the trade it had been; he had himself taken to the road at the early age of fifteen, having been persuaded to that industry by an uncle of his, a Canon of Viterbo. " For in the old days " (he was careful to add) " this country was very easily administered, and the clergy in especial defended and encouraged the picturesque customs which such an ease of administration bred. Often after a hard

The Brigand of Radicofani

night upon the highway, or after some successful
business in the brushwood above the city, I would
make it my business to call upon my revered uncle
to press upon him some trinket as a mark of my
esteem, or if the day had been exceptionally lucky,
some piece of foreign gold which a tourist (for they
were even then numerous in these parts) might have
left in my possession. The old man died," continued
the Brigand with a sigh, "in the year '68, during
the reign of the late Pope Pius IX, and it was
perhaps as well, for great changes were impending
which, had he lived to see them, would have broken his
heart. For myself," the Brigand went on thoughtfully, "I am too much of a patriot to complain of
the unification of my country, and I had some hopes
on the establishment of a new government of obtain-
ing a permanent situation under it which, as I was
now approaching middle age, would be more consonant to my years than the precarious though active
and healthy career I had hitherto pursued. For
some moments in the year 1873 I hoped I might be
appointed receiver of the taxes, a post for which my
intimate knowledge of the whole countryside and
my many connections with the farmers of the locality
seemed singularly to fit me. A former chief of
mine, for whom I had always preserved a reverent
attachment, was very powerful in this department,
and assured me that I might look for a regular post
so soon as he was himself installed in the office of
the Fisc at Orvieto. But there '" continued the

On Anything

Brigand, sighing, " loyalty and gratitude are senti-
ments soon dissipated in the atmosphere of politics,
and though I had the pleasure of seeing my old
chief installed as the head of his department, no
such post as he had hinted at came my way.   Meanwhile trade sank : artists, literary men, and poor
fowl of that sort still thought it an eccentric and
therefore a desirable thing to approach the Eternal
City by road, and these I would not infrequently be
at the pains of carrying off for ransom ; but it was a
dwindling and a most unsatisfactory trade.   The
wealthy took more and more to the railway ; the new
government at the Quirinal, after a certain amount
of hesitation, definitely decided upon a policy inimical
to our profession, if not actually hostile to it.   My
advancing years, and the various circumstances I
have detailed, made the dear old life less and less
possible, until one day " (here he sighed again profoundly) " in '93, just ten years ago, I was constrained
to accept a situation as a model under an agency
which provides such individuals for the entertainment of foreigners.   I was already old (I am over
seventy as you see me here and now), but I often
think with bitterness as I poise upon one leg in an
attitude of flight, or shield my eyes with my hands
with a gesture that is very much applauded by the
ladies who sketch me—I often think with bitterness,
I say, as I adopt these various attitudes to order, of
the days when I was known as the Lion of the
Amiata, when my name was a terror from   far
190

beyond the Tiber to the marshes that border the Mediterranean Sea."

The old man was silent, and the journalist, who had been busy taking notes, and was profoundly moved by the recital he had heard, asked the Brigand most deferentially and in a gentle tone whether these memories did not stir him to some particular story, and whether he could not recite before the stranger left some especially telling incident of his great past.

" Why," mused the vigorous old man, rising slowly from his chair, " I think I can reconstruct for you that famous occasion which the old wives still tell as a winter story, when I held up the Syndic of Montefiascone, and without the trouble of binding him to a tree nor of inflicting the slightest mutilation, I acquired for the purposes of my expenditure all that was movable upon his person. Come, let us reconstruct the scene." He put a heavy hand upon the young journalist's shoulder, looking round the room as he did so for a favourable stage upon which to order the drama.

The Colonial rose at the same time, and the Brigand, shaking his head, and growling like a monarch of the forest, muttered deeply: " No, no, this place is too small ! "

With the moving of the chairs many had come into the little inn parlour and followed the pair out into the blazing market square, and the brigand led the now dubious journalist into that public place.

191

On Anything

Their appearance in the open was the signal for a great gathering ; children ran from narrow alleys, market women rushed up with shrill voices, farmers engaged in bargaining left their sport for the superior attractions of the scene, and loud cries of " The Brigand is going to work—come and see the Brigand " were heard upon every side. The journalist maintained his dignity, and even allowed a faint smile to flicker upon his anxious lips as the Brigand, pacing the cobblestones of the market-place in a thoughtful manner, decided the spot where his companion should stand.

" Here," he said, stamping with his foot, " this was about the distance."

The journalist found himself alone, the crowd retired at some fifty yards ; before him was the street leading northward out of the town towards Sienna ; it was empty. He turned and saw facing him the large concourse of people recounting to each other the interest of the proceedings ; and he further perceived that the Brigand, who stood a little in front of them all, was slowly disembarrassing his blunder-buss from the innumerable details of his costume.

" Thus," shouted the old giant in a terrible voice, " stood I. There where you are stood the Syndic. Come, look slightly away and upwards as though you did not perceive me, for such was the Syndic's atti-tude upon the occasion in question. Make as though you were walking leisurely, but do not actually take a step, for that would destroy the reconstruction of the scene which I am arranging for your entertainment."

With great deliberation the Brigand of Radicofani next proceeded to pour into the huge bell mouth of his blunderbuss a measure of gunpowder from a horn ; next he rammed in a piece of the anticlerical newspaper with the rusty ramrod which he had with difficulty drawn from its rings ; he replaced the ramrod, and as deliberately dropped into the mouth of his deadly instrument a number of large leaden slugs.

"Thus," said he as he made these preparations, "did I carefully load while the unsuspecting Syndic leisurely crossed before my line of fire."

As he said these words the Brigand slowly raised the blunderbuss to his shoulder, leaned his great body forward, and bent his head until an eye of extraordinary brilliance and power was gleaming down the top of the barrel. The concourse was now silent, and the journalist, with an admirable sense of what was required of him, adopted the attitude of a man walking at a leisurely pace, and acted to perfection the part of the Syndic.

"Halt!" roared the Brigand in startling and quite novel tones. The journalist instinctively started, and the Brigand bitterly added : "Must I fire, or will you spare me that expense by laying carefully upon the ground at your feet your watch, your purse, your rings, your pocket-book, and such valuables as you may have about you ? "

On Anything

The journalist with no little hesitation (for he found this too realistic) threw down a coin by way of *simulacrum*.

"He mocks me!" bellowed the Brigand, while all the crowd applauded. "He hesitates to obey (thus did I speak to the Syndic). Come, empty all your pockets and turn them inside out that I may see them."

The journalist, excusing his pride by the reflection that the whole thing was but a game, with some reluctance did as he was bid. There lay at his feet upon the market square of Radicofani a little heap of valuables, a quantity of private correspondence, a handkerchief and a note-book.

"Now," shouted the Brigand, still carefully aiming at the foreigner's head, "go! Go warily, and step backward if you choose, to assure yourself that I shall not lower my gun."

For some few steps the journalist so walked toward the northern gate, and step by step, keeping his distance, the immense old man pursued, while the crowd with subdued applause, encouraged his action, and with rising menaces bade the stranger not cross the Brigand's purpose, since upon these occasions he was terrible if he was thwarted. When he had nearly reached the limits of the town the unfortunate traveller began to protest that the joke should end. To his horror the reply which reached him, not from the Brigand alone but from many of his supporters, was given in tones of increasing sincerity, and he

The Brigand of Radicofani

shuddered to see, or to think he saw, the pressure of the finger upon the trigger. He hesitated for a moment, and then suddenly he ran. . . .

The northern road out of Radicofani is steep: its steepness aided his flight, and when he was well down toward the valley he heard (and that increased his determination) a loud report, and high over his head sung a covey of slugs. He neither looked back nor attempted to order his confused mind, but ran without ceasing until from sheer exhaustion he dropped at the roadside.

To his delight he saw two mounted policemen in splendid uniforms. He recounted his tale ; they looked at him severely, and one of them, beckoning with his finger, said, " Follow us."

He followed them for miles and miles. Of how he was subsequently examined, disbelieved, threatened with fine and imprisonment, and at last escaped only by an appeal to his consul in Sienna, you may read in the interesting memoirs which he is about to publish under the title of " Etruscan Wine and Song."

Meanwhile in Radicofani the Brigand drinks and sings.

THE HONEST MAN AND THE DEVIL

A MAN who prided himself very justly upon his uncompromising temper and love of truth had the misfortune the other night to wake at about three o'clock in the morning and to see the Devil standing by his bedside, who begged him that he (the Honest Man) should sell him (the Devil) his soul.

" I will do nothing of the kind," said the Honest Man in a mixture of sleepiness and alarm.

" Very well," said the Devil, quite obviously put out, " you shall go your own way ; but I warn you, if you will have nothing to do with me I will have nothing to do with you ! "

" I ask for nothing better," said the Honest Man, turning over on his right side to get to sleep again, " I desire to follow Truth in all her ways, and to have nothing more to do with you." With these words he began a sort of regular and mechanical breathing which warned the Devil that the interview was now at an end. The Devil, therefore, with a grunt, went out of the bedroom and shut the door smartly behind him, shaking all the furniture ; which

The Honest Man and the Devil

was a rude thing to do, but he was very much annoyed.

Next morning the Honest Man, before going out to business, dictated his letters as was his wont into a phonograph ; this little instrument (which, by the way, had been invented by the Devil though he did not know it) is commonly used in the houses of the busy for the reception of dictated correspondence, comic verse, love sonnets, and so forth ; and if the busy also live by their pen, the phonograph spares them the use of this instrument. The Honest Man of whom I speak had no such profession ; he used the phonograph for his daily correspondence, which was enormous ; he dictated his answers into it before leaving his private house, and during the forenoon his secretary would take down those answers by reversing the machine and putting it at a slower pace so that what it said could easily go down upon the typewriter.

At about half-past five the Honest Man came back from his business, and was met by his secretary in a very nervous fashion.

" I fear, sir," said the secretary, "that there must be some mistake about your correspondence. I have taken it down literally as was my duty, and certainly the voice sounded like yours, but the letters are hardly such as I would post without your first reading them. I have therefore forborne to sign them in your name, and have kept them to show you upon your return. Here they are. Pray, pray read them in seclusion, and advise me at the earliest moment." With these words the secretary handed the documents to his bewildered employer, and went out of the room with his eyes full of nervous tears.

The Honest Man put on a pair of gold spectacles, exchanged these for some gold pince-nez, hummed twice, then began to read. This is what he read—

I

The Laurels,
Putney Heath, S. W.
November 9.

DEAR LADY WHERNSIDE,

Yes, I will come to Whernside House next Thursday. I do not know you well, and I shall feel out of place among your friends, but I need not stop long. I think that to be seen at such a gathering, even for but a few moments, is of general advantage to my business; otherwise I should certainly not come. One thing I beg of you, which is that you will not ask me a number of private questions under the illusion that you are condescending. The habit is very offensive to me, and it is the chief drawback I feel in visiting your house. I may add that though I am of the middle classes, like your late father, I have a very pretty taste in furniture, and the inside of your house simply makes me sick.

I am,

Very faithfully yours,

JOHN ROE.

The Honest Man and the Devil

II

The Laurels,
Putney Heath, S. W.
November 9.

DEAR SIR,

No; I will not entertain your proposal to use the Imperial British Suction Apparatus upon my ships. It may be a very good apparatus, and it might possibly increase my profits by £2000 in the year, but the fact is that I am so well to do it is hardly worth my while to bother about these little things. The bother of arranging the new installation, and the risk that, after all, my men might not know how to use it, has decided me. I note what you say, that the French, the German, the Italian, the Russian, and the United States Governments have all bought your patent for use in their Navies; but it does not influence me one jot. What are they, after all, but foreigners? Besides which, it is my experience that somehow or other I muddle through, and I hate having to think.

We are,

Your obedient Servants,

JOHN ROE & COMPANY.

III

The Laurels,
Putney Heath, S. W.
November 9.

DEAR DOCTOR BURTON,

I wish you would come round this afternoon or to-morrow morning and see my eldest child,

On Anything

James.   There is nothing whatever the matter with
him, but his mother is in a flurry, because some
children with whom he went out to a party the
other evening have developed mumps, and his voice
is husky, which she idiotically believes to be a
symptom of that disease.   Your visit will cost me
two guineas ; but it is well worth my while to spend
that sum if only to avoid her intolerable fussing.
My advice to you as man to man is, to look at the
child's tongue, give him some plain water by way of
medicine, and go off again as quick as you can.
Your fee will be the same in any case, and it is
ridiculous to waste time over such business.

I am,

Your sincere friend,

JOHN ROE.

IV

The Laurels,
Putney Heath, S. W.
November 9.

DEAR DOCTOR MILLS,

I enclose five guineas and a subscription
for your new church.   I confess that I do not clearly
see what advantage this expenditure will do me, and
I should have some hesitancy in setting down in
black and white my reasons for sending you the
money at all.   Your style of preaching is monotonous, your doctrines (if they are really your
doctrines) are particularly offensive to me ; and after
all we could get along perfectly well with the old

200

The Honest Man and the Devil

church. At bottom I think this kind of thing is a
sort of blackmail; you know I cannot afford to have
my name left out of your subscription list, and
probably the same motive is causing many another
sensible neighbour of mine to part most reluctantly
with a portion of his property. Perhaps the best
way out of it would be to form a sort of union and
to strike all together against your exactions; but I
cannot be at the pains of wasting any more time
upon the matter, so here's your five guineas and be
hanged to you!

Very faithfully and respectfully yours,

JOHN ROE.

V

The Laurels,
Putney Heath, S. W.
November 9.

DEAR SIR,

I have received your estimate for the
new conservatory; I have figured it out and
undoubtedly you will lose upon the contract. I
therefore accept it without reserve and beg you to
begin work as soon as possible. I fully appreciate
your motive in making so extraordinary a bargain :
you know that I shall make further alterations to
the house, and you hope by throwing away a sprat
to catch a whale. Do not imagine that I shall be
misled in this regard. The next alteration I have

to make I will accept the tender of some other builder as gullible as yourself, and so forth to the end of the chapter.   And I am,

Your obedient servant,

JOHN ROE.

VI

The Laurels,
Putney Heath, S. W.
November 9.

MY DEAR ALICE,

I will not send the small sum which you ask me as a brother to afford you, though I am well aware that it would save you very poignant anxiety. My reason for acting thus is that a little annoyance is caused me when I have to disburse even a small sum without the chance of any possible return, and especially when I have to do it to benefit some one who cannot make things uncomfortable for me if I refuse.   I have a sort of sentimental feeling about you, because you are my sister, and to that extent my refusal does give me a slight, though a passing sense of irrision.   But that will very soon disappear, and when I balance it against the definite sacrifice of a sum of money, however small, I do not hesitate for a moment.   Please do not write to me again.

Your affectionate brother,

JOHN ROE.

The Honest Man and the Devil

VII

The Laurels,
Putney Heath, S. W.
November 9.

DEAR SIR,

I enclose a cheque for £250, my annual subscription to the local War Chest of the Party. I beg you particularly to note that this subscription makes me the creditor of the Party to the extent of over £3000, counting interest at one above bank rate from the first subscription. I have carefully gone into this and there can be no error. I would further have you note that I desire no reward or recognition for my disbursement of this sum beyond the baronetcy of which we spoke the last time I visited you, in the presence of a third party; and I must conclude by assuring you that any lengthy negotiation would be extremely distasteful to me. You need not fear my attitude in the approaching election; I am quite indifferent to parliamentary honours, I will take the chair five times and no more; I am good for one large garden party, three dinners, and a set of fireworks. I will have absolutely nothing to do with the printing, and I am,

Always at your service,

JOHN ROE.

When the Honest Man had perused these letters he decided that they should not be posted in their present form; but upon attempting to amend them he found himself singularly lacking in those phrases which he could usually discover so readily for the purposes of his correspondence.

He sent, therefore, for his secretary, and told him to re-write the letters himself according to his own judgment, which that gentleman did with singular skill and dispatch, maintaining the cheques as drafted and putting every matter in its proper light.

That night the Honest Man, who was sleeping soundly, was more annoyed than ever at the reappearance of the Devil at his bedside in the middle of the night.

"Now," said the Devil, "have I brought you to your senses?"

"No," said the Honest Man, composing himself for sleep as before, "you have not. You should have remembered that I have a secretary."

"Oh, the devil!" said the Devil impatiently, "one cannot be thinking of everything!" And he went out even more noisily than the night before.

In this way the Honest Man saved his soul and at the same time his face, which, if it were the less valuable of the two organs, was none the less of considerable moment to him in this mundane sphere.

COMPIEGNE

[*The Main Room over the Terrace of the Palace in Compiègne. An autumn night in* 1782. *The room is lit with many candles, and there is dancing. The Queen of France is present, the Court, and some few of the neighbouring gentry, among whom a Lady called Madame d'Escurolles, about forty, silent, and rather timid. A gentleman about the Court, a trifle older than herself, stands by and talks to her as she sits and looks at the dancing. He takes his title from Noirétable in the Forèz, but he has never been there.*]

MADAME D'ESCUROLLES. I cannot see anything in the Queen of what you say, M. de Noirétable. She seems to be a little violent, but not vulgar.

MONSIEUR DE NOIRÉTABLE. It is precisely as you will, but I confess she spoils a room for me. The truth is that if she jostled and elbowed she would please me better; she always looks as though she would. I am disappointed in my amusement.

MADAME D'ESCUROLLES. M. de Noirétable, she is a good woman. I can see it in her eyes. They are very frank.

205

On Anything

MONSIEUR DE NOIRÉTABLE. Oh! Yes! Madame, they are frank enough. They are being frank just now to half the room. Ugh! I have seen market women looking so, but only at the return from market (*he pauses*). Have you ridden to-day?

MADAME D'ESCUROLLES (*laughing gently*). No, sir, I have not ridden. We do not ride at my age in Compiègne . . . but, tell me, do you not think there is something majestic about the Queen? . . . You must remember I have not seen her for three years, and it may be you are used to her carriage. But do you not admire that poise of the head and that high manner; or perhaps I should say, have you not admired them?

MONSIEUR DE NOIRÉTABLE. Oh! yes, Madame, I have admired it, and I do, as also her hairdresser and her shoemaker. Am I not at Court?

MADAME D'ESCUROLLES. But they say it is at Court that she is least admired?

MONSIEUR DE NOIRÉTABLE (*shocked*). I would not presume to say that! God forbid! From what I have heard in the street I would say she was least admired in Paris, or, perhaps—(*musing*)—perhaps in the village of Louveciennes . . . nay, I have forgotten St. Cloud. St. Cloud would run Louveciennes hard.

MADAME D'ESCUROLLES. I have do doubt these names are well known in Versailles.

MONSIEUR DE NOIRÉTABLE. Madame, Versailles knows everything and everybody, because Versailles is the Queen. For myself, after many years in the full view of Versailles and taking my money from Versailles, yet I cannot say I like Versailles.

MADAME D'ESCUROLLES (*innocently*). And why not, sir?

MONSIEUR DE NOIRÉTABLE (*looking vaguely at the distant candles and speaking as vaguely*). Upon my soul I cannot say! . . . It may be that Versailles is too frank or perhaps there is too much poise about it . . . it is certainly majestic.

MADAME D'ESCUROLLES (*as though merely to continue*) It must compare well with poor Compiègne!

MONSIEUR DE NOIRÉTABLE (*ceasing to look at the candles*). I would not compare Versailles with Compiègne because I have seen Versailles so much and Compiègne so little. Indeed, Madame (if you will believe me!), I have but twice visited Compiègne since my year in garrison there, but that was fifteen years ago, and in those days, as you will remember, it was your father who befriended me. I found Compiègne very hospitable, and if I have returned there too seldom I very readily acknowledge my error.

MADAME D'ESCUROLLES (*as though to change the subject*). Pray, sir, do you not find Compiègne much older? They say that age particularly affects Compiègne.

MONSIEUR DE NOIRÉTABLE (*with a little humour*). I know that *I* have aged, but I would not swear for Compiègne. Madame d'Escurolles (*with enthusiasm*),

On Anything

I cannot forbear to tell you that Compiègne in my eyes does not age, but grows. The walls of Compiègne are more subtle and her woods more deep ; her air is more gracious and full of certitude and peace than in those days I speak of when she held me for a full year.

MADAME D'ESCUROLLES. Oh ! *Held* you, Monsieur de Noirétable ! You were under no constraint. It was your garrison.

MONSIEUR DE NOIRÉTABLE (*rapidly*). Madame, my youth was held. But I have not told you all of my own ageing nor of this return to Compiègne. . . . You say the town has aged also. Ah ! You should see other towns ! There is in Compiègne to-day, I swear to you, more deep and more desirable laughter than in the youngest and most virginal of towns !

MADAME D'ESCUROLLES. Why, M. de Noirétable, you grow lyrical ! (*Smiling.*) One would think you had seen too many towns !

MONSIEUR DE NOIRÉTABLE (*lightly and rapidly*). A man in the Service must see many towns. . . . It is not wholly his choice. I volunteered as well, and saw more towns than I positively needed, Madame ; to tell the truth, a man is none the better for visiting too many towns.

MADAME D'ESCUROLLES. It is the appetite for travel, Monsieur, and the love of adventure.

MONSIEUR DE NOIRÉTABLE. Precisely, Madame, you put it very well . . . the appetite, Madame, and the love . . . of adventure . . . you put it very well indeed. (*Abruptly.*) It led me to Narbonne, to Florac, and to Cahors.

MADAME D'ESCUROLLES (*shuddering*). Oh! Monsieur de Noirétable! What dreadful names!

MONSIEUR DE NOIRÉTABLE (*lightly*). Not at all, Madame! Not at all! Delightful! . . . but passing, very passing! Believe me, in the presence of Compiègne, no man desires to return to Florac or to Narbonne, nor even to Cahors.

MADAME D'ESCUROLLES. No . . . but he may choose to visit other places.

MONSIEUR DE NOIRÉTABLE (*gravely*). He may be compelled to visit them, Madame. (*She looks away.*)

MADAME D'ESCUROLLES (*is silent for a little while and then looks up at him as gravely*). *Must* he visit so many towns?

MONSIEUR DE NOIRÉTABLE (*slightly lifting his shoulders*). Oh! Must! Must! Must is a strong word, Madame. But *Does, Does; does* is a working word, Madame. And a man *does* visit many towns, and he comes back to Compiègne.

MADAME D'ESCUROLLES (*thoughtfully*). Sir, Compiègne has age upon it, though you are pleased to call it by prettier names. Compiègne is even sad with age. I will not deny her charm, I will even concede her beauty—but it is harder than ever to-day to be content with Compiègne. (*With a sudden change of tone.*) We have spoken too much of cities. We old friends who do not dance treat the place too much like a card-room, and we converse when younger souls are full of the music. . . . Tell me, Monsieur de Noirétable—since the subject is more consonant with music and with dancing—are you fond of verse ?

MONSIEUR DE NOIRÉTABLE (*solemnly*). I dote upon it ! especially such verse as may be written in praise of Compiègne. . . .

MADAME D'ESCUROLLES (*laughing*). Oh ! Monsieur de Noirétable, you begin to be ridiculous. Come, is there no verse you may cite as your favourite ?

MONSIEUR DE NOIRÉTABLE. Why, Madame, I fear to seem even more ridiculous if I quote Latin.

MADAME D'ESCUROLLES (*good-humouredly*). Not at all, sir ! We know Latin in Compiègne !

MONSIEUR DE NOIRÉTABLE (*grimly*). So I seemed to remember. Well, then, I confess my favourite verse is the Horatian Ode which begins—

> Donec gratus eram tibi . . .

and which ends (*he speaks glowingly*)—

> . . Iracundior Hadria
> Tecum vivere amem ; tecum obeam libens !

MADAME D'ESCUROLLES (*doubtfully*). Are you quite sure you have the Latin right ? (*She ponders awhile.*) For my own part I prefer the simple songs of our own people about here and the rhymes of children. Do you know

> Nous n'irons plus aux bois
> Les lauriers sont coupés ?

Compiègne

MONSIEUR DE NOIRÉTABLE (*almost yawning*). Oh!
Bless you, yes. Who does not. . . . Madame?

(*The music ceases and the reverences to the Queen
begin. Madame d'Escurolles, as she moves forward,
says in a low tone to Monsieur de Noirétable as she
passes him,* "When do you next come to
Compiègne?")

MONSIEUR DE NOIRÉTABLE (*as he goes out alone, to
himself*). When Compiègne comes to meet me half-
way; which is perhaps a little difficult for so much
stone.

THE CANDOUR OF MATURITY

(*The Marquis* DE LA MISE-EN-SCÈNE *is discovered
writing at a little inlaid table.   He is about* 42 *years
of age, and looks worse than that.   He believes himself to be alone in the room, when he is somewhat
suddenly addressed from the open door by the Duchess*
DE LA TOUR-DE-FORCE, *who has just entered.   She is
a woman of about* 55, *somewhat too commanding.   The
place is Versailles, and the time is* 1753.)

THE DUCHESS DE LA TOUR-DE-FORCE. What are you
doing, Monsieur de la Mise-en-Scène?

THE MARQUIS DE LA MISE-EN-SCÈNE (*continuing to
write and without turning round*). I am writing, Duchess,
as you can plainly see.

DUCHESS. Unfortunately I cannot see through your
body, but I see you are seated at a table, and from
the constrained attitude of your elbow and the
awkward wagging of your head I can well believe
that you are occupied as you say.

THE MARQUIS (*without turning round*). Come,
Duchess, would you have me jump up like a bour-
geois?   Shall I ask after your health, which I know

The Candour of Maturity

to be robust, or murmur something polite about your niece ?   Shall I come and hold the door for you, or do any of those things to which you are used in provincial hotels ?   Or shall I go on writing ?   (*He goes on writing.*) (*A pause.*) (*The* Duchess *walks into the room, shuts the door rather noisily, and sits down upon a chair. She sighs.*)

The Marquis (*still writing, murmuring to himself*). " Indifferent " !   Tut, tut, how does one spell " indifferent " ?   " You cannot be indifferent to my plea " . . . " plea." . . . I know how to spell " plea," but how does one spell " indifferent " ? (*Turning round for the first time to the Duchess and showing a set, half-ironical face, with thin lips and steady grey eyes.*) Duchess, how do you spell " indifferent " ?

Duchess (*carelessly*). Oh, I spell it sometimes one way, sometimes another. But I believe there are two f's.

Marquis (*turning again to his letters*). " Indifferent " (with two f's) " to my plea. . . ." (*He leans back and looks at the paper with his head on one side as though he were examining a picture.*) It looks all right, Duchess.   I always go by that, though I think it is easier to tell whether a bit of spelling is right if you can see it in print.

Duchess (*gravely*). I thoroughly agree with you, Marquis de la Mise-en-Scène. (*A pause during which the scratching of the quill continues.*)   I do not think she will mind about the spelling ; but if I know anything of her sex she will not read the end of the letter if you make it too long.

MARQUIS (*still writing away busily*). Yes, she will, for it is full of business.

DUCHESS (*with some interest in her voice*). Why? What kind of business?

MARQUIS. I'm writing a proposal of marriage, Madam.

DUCHESS (*really startled*). Good heavens, Monsieur de la Mise-en-Scène! I always thought you were married!

MARQUIS (*continuing to write*). Madame de la Tour-de-Force, that is the malicious sort of thing people say at Versailles about provincials. (*He continues to write.*)

DUCHESS. I don't care how much business you put into it; if you make it as long as that she won't read to the end.

MARQUIS. Oh, yes, she will. The letter isn't very long, but I'm writing it out several times.

DUCHESS. Really! Your cynicism! And suppose the various ladies meet, or suppose two of them accept you at once! What then?

MARQUIS (*getting up quickly*). I never thought of that! (*He puts his left hand on to the hilt of his sword, puts his right hand to his chin, and thoughtfully paces up and down the room.*) Yes, Duchess, that would be very awkward. In fact (*going to the window and looking out*)—in fact, now that you have suggested it . . . of course I might write to the second and

The Candour of Maturity

say I already had an engagement . . . but I think I shall drive tandem and not send off the second letter until I have received an answer to the first; nor the third until I have received an answer to the second, and so forth . . . On the other hand, I'm glad I've got the work done, because the business part at the end is very complicated.

DUCHESS (*as though to make conversation*). Have you ever written a proposal of marriage before, Monsieur de la Mise-en-Scène?

MARQUIS. No, Duchess, I have not; and, what is more curious, no lady has ever shown me one. But I have a book in which various forms of letters are set down to be used upon different occasions in life. I have taken all the first part of this letter of mine from this book. The long part at the end which is all about business I got out of a letter from my solicitor.

DUCHESS (*quietly, as she folds her hands upon her lap*). If you will take my advice, Marquis, you will not put in so much business upon the very first occasion. I should have asked—Have you actually met any of these ladies?

MARQUIS (*stoutly*). Yes, all of them, and one of them three or four times. Tell me, Duchess, since you know something of the world, in what form is a declaration most pleasing?

DUCHESS (*serenely*). By word of mouth, Monsieur de la Mise-en-Scène.

MARQUIS. Oh, by word of mouth! And under

what conditions ? On horseback ? During a gentle stroll ? In a ball-room ?

DUCHESS. No, rather under the conditions of ordinary life, in an ordinary room such as this, in the midst of one's ordinary avocations.

MARQUIS (*stops in his pacing up and down, stands near her, and, looking at her fixedly, says*) : I attach the greatest possible value to your judgment and advice, Duchess. And I fear I have wasted a good deal of time writing those letters at the little table. Here is an ordinary room, here are we both at our ordinary avocations, which consist in doing nothing, now sauntering up and down the floors, now sitting upon chairs ; all is as you would desire it. We are not on horseback, we are not at a ball, we are not strolling through the park. Will you marry me ?

DUCHESS (*composedly*). Certainly not !

MARQUIS. Oh, well then, I'm very glad I did write those letters after all. It's a great thing to have one's work behind one instead of in front of one. But before I get to the tedious task again I do particularly beg you to consider my proposal. (*He sits down in a chair opposite her and begins to tick off the fingers of his left hand with the forefinger of his right.*) My first point is this——

DUCHESS (*wearily*). Oh, Monsieur de la Mise-en-Scène, are you going to put it under three heads ?

MARQUIS. No, Madam, I act in this fashion because I have seen the attitude adopted invariably by all diplomats when they would convince some great

and powerful Sovereign ; and my first point is this :
We know each other and we know the world. On
the other hand, we are not intimate friends, which
would be fatal. We are both free. We are both
careless as to differences in rank.

DUCHESS. I am not.

MARQUIS. Well, well, let us pass that : it is a
matter one can soon get used to after the first years
of married life.

DUCHESS. I assure you, you are wasting your time.
I have not the slightest intention of marrying you
or anybody else. But I will help you to get
married if you like. My advice will be useful to
you, as you say. And, first of all, show me those
letters.

MARQUIS (*warmly*). Thank you, Madam ; thank you
a thousand times ! This one here is to Madame de
Livaudan (*hands her one letter and holds the other ready
in his hand*).

DUCHESS (*glancing at it*). It is too formal !

MARQUIS. This one (*he hands her another*) is to an
Italian lady, whose name I will get hold of before
I write the direction outside ; for the moment it
escapes me, but she is a Contessa, something like
Marolio, and I met her in a coach.

DUCHESS (*reads it*). It is far too long.

MARQUIS. This one (*he hands her a third*) is to a
distant cousin of mine in Madrid, formerly the wife
of——

DUCHESS (*in surprise*). But are they all widows ?

On Anything

MARQUIS (*gravely*). Yes, Madam, they are all widows—and all rich.

DUCHESS (*sighing profoundly*). It certainly seems a pity that with your knowledge of Versailles and your pleasant habit of friendship . . . and your gallant record in the war . . . you should be compelled to such adventures.

MARQUIS (*lightly*). There! there! Madam, do not pity me. Many a poor fellow is worse off than I. The fourth one . . . (*He produces yet another letter.*)

DUCHESS (*waving it aside*). No, no, I have already seen too much of that correspondence! Trust me, Marquis, it will all end in smoke, and may even very possibly make you ridiculous.

MARQUIS (*apologetically*). Madam, I have done my best. I have put before you the very reasonable proposal that we should marry. I put it before you in the very manner which you suggest. It did not, for the moment at least, meet with your approval: and surely it was common-sense to keep my line of retreat open upon the four widows, by any one of which roads I might have fallen back after my defeat at your hands.

DUCHESS (*thoughtfully*). No, I do not think we should get married. There are too many doubts. . . . I have seen such experiments fail . . . and (*shrugging her shoulders*) succeed . . . I confess I have seen them fail and succeed.

MARQUIS. Indeed?

DUCHESS (*still ruminating, but in a quiet way*). Yes.

218

The Candour of Maturity

. . . On one's own land. . . . Yes, that is how it always has to begin. And then there would be the getting of a post (*she still continues to think it over, frowning with the interest of her subject; at last she rises promptly, and looking the Marquis full in the face she says*): We have half-an-hour or more before the hunt comes home. We will walk round the gardens together and give this very important matter the discussion it deserves.

MARQUIS (*cheerfully*). By all means, Duchess, so that you do not make me miss the courier who is to take the first of these missives. I am entirely at your disposal.

DUCHESS. It is my deliberate advice to you not to post the first of those letters to-day. Come! (*She goes out of the door in a rather majestic manner, and he follows, smiling.*)

THE FOG

(A young man in the uniform of a Lieutenant of Dragoons is riding on the edge of a wood in a thick fog. The month is the month of November, and the year is the year 1793. The young man has a simple, open face, with rather protuberant blue eyes and sandy hair. His mouth is at a half smile, and he does not seem to mind having lost his way. His name is Boutroux.)

BOUTROUX. The more I see of warfare the more I am astonished ! . . . It is true I have only seen four months of it. . . . My father would be very much astonished if he could see me now ! . . . My mother would be more than astonished : she would be positively alarmed ! On the other hand (*musing*) it is a great relief to me, and would be a still greater relief to her, that I cannot hear the sound of fire-arms. . . . The more I see of warfare the more and more perplexed I become. (*Looking up at the edge of the wood on his left.*) Now what is that wood ? Before the fog fell I could have sworn we were in an open rolling country with spinneys here and

220

The Fog

there, and I could almost have told you very roughly where we were and where the enemy were—more or less—so to speak—and now here is a horrid great wood! And where am I?

(*At this moment a single voice is heard through the fog. The single voice belongs to a man called* METRIS. *He is as yet unseen.*)

METRIS. Get back a little! When I said follow me I did not mean bunching up like a lot of dirty linesmen. I meant keeping your spaces. . . . Charles, you are as pig-headed as ever! There are times when one does not answer a superior, but there are other times when one does. (*Angrily.*) Charles! (*There is no reply.*) Something has gone very definitely wrong with my troop! That is the worst of fog.

(*As he says this he emerges in a vast and murky way into the vision of Boutroux. The two men stop their horses and look at each other through the mist.*)

BOUTROUX. Have you seen the Thirty-second?

METRIS. (*Boutroux perceives him to be a tall man quite ten years his senior, very lean, with menacing moustaches, and clothed in a uniform with which he is unfamiliar.*) No, sir, I have not seen the Thirty-second. (*He salutes with a sword.*) I take it you are an officer in the Republican service?

BOUTROUX (*wearily*). Oh yes!

METRIS (*with elaborate courtesy*). Then, sir, you

221

On Anything

are my prisoner! My name is Georges de Metris, of Heyren in this country, and my father's name will be familiar to you.

BOUTROUX. Your father's name is not familiar to me, sir. And what is more, *my* father's name would not be familiar to you. For my poor old dad (God bless him!) is at the present moment in Bayonne, where he is a grocer—in a large way of business, I am glad to say. And talking of prisoners, you are my prisoner! It is as well I should tell you this before we go further. For if there is one thing I detest more than another in this new profession of mine it is the ambiguity thereof. (*He salutes with his sword in rather an extravagant fashion and smiles broadly.*)

METRIS (*making his horse trot up quite close to* BOUTROUX *and halting stiffly while he lowers his sword*). Sir! I should be loath to quarrel with one so young and evidently so new to arms.

BOUTROUX. And I, sir (*lowering his sword as far as ever he can stretch*), would be still more loath to quarrel with one so greatly my senior and one evidently too used to this lethal game.

METRIS (*biting his lips*). I detest your principles, sir, but I respect your uniform.

BOUTROUX. You have the advantage of me, sir. Your uniform seems to me positively grotesque. But your principles I admire enormously.

METRIS (*stiffly*). Sir, I serve the Emperor. You have heard my name.

BOUTROUX. I have heard your name, and now that

222

you tell me that you serve the Emperor I am willing to believe *that* also. So it seems that we are enemies. I thought as much when you first showed out of the fog. It was not your uniform which gave me this opinion.

METRIS. Then what is it?

BOUTROUX. It was your singular habit of commanding men who were not there.

METRIS (*in a boiling passion, which he restrains*). I did not come here, sir, for a contest of words.

BOUTROUX (*genially, putting up his sword*). I take it you did not come here with any direct motive. You got here somehow, just as I did, and neither of us knows why.

METRIS (*in extreme anger*). But you will know why very soon, sir ! And I hope I shall know why, too ! Sir, I call upon you to draw !

BOUTROUX (*seating himself back in the saddle with great ease while his horse munches the wet grass*). Now, there you are. I have been a soldier only these few weeks, and I thought I had got hold of all the muddlement there was ; " lines " which aren't lines, and " positions strongly held " which anybody can walk round for fun ; and communications " cut," when, as a fact, one could go right along them on horseback, and " destructive fire " that hits nobody, and " excellent moral " when one's men are on the point of hitting one on the nose. But if you will allow me, sir, you positively take the prize in the matter ! You suggest the duello or some such phantasy. Do you want us to fight with these cavalry swords from the saddle ?

METRIS. I do not know if you are trying to gain time, sir. I suggest that you should meet me on foot here and now.

BOUTROUX. What ! and lose my horse ?

METRIS. Sir, we can tie the two beasts by their bridles, and we can hang their bridles so tied to the branch of one of these trees.

BOUTROUX (*frowning*). I have a very short experience of warfare—I think I have said that before—and I hesitate to correct a man of your experience. But if you can really *tie* two bridles together and then have enough leather left to get it over the branch of a tree, you'll teach me something about the art of campaigning of which I was quite innocent. . . . (*Getting down from his horse.*) Come, I think in the French service we have a better way than that. (*He unbuckles one end of the snaffle-rein.*) You see (*looking up genially*), we leave the curb on. If I had time I would explain to you why. . . . Now, sir, will you not unbuckle the end of your snaffle-rein ?

METRIS (*stiffly*). No, sir, I will not.

BOUTROUX (*sighing*). They are all the same ! The service simply fossilises them, especially, it would seem, the enemy ; though I confess (*turning courteously to* METRIS *and bowing to him*) you are the first of the enemy I have ever met.

METRIS (*restraining himself*). Pray, sir, do not delay.

BOUTROUX (*full of good humour*). I will not ! See,

The Fog

I pass my snaffle-rein in through the buckle of your horse's curb; and pardon me, sir, but what a fine horse! Is it yours or the Emperor's?

METRIS (*ominously*). It is mine, sir.

BOUTROUX. Keep it. This (*jerking his thumb at his weedy mount*) belongs to the Republic—if it is still a Republic, for news travels slowly to the armies. At any rate, it doesn't belong to me. (*He slowly takes the end of his snaffle-rein and looks for something to fasten it to; he shakes his head doubtfully. At last, holding the end of the snaffle-rein in his left hand while the two horses begin to browse peacefully, he draws his sword with his right, and putting himself in a theatrical posture, says*): Come on, sir, I'm damned if I will let go of these horses.

METRIS (*solemnly*). I do not jest upon these occasions.

BOUTROUX. Neither do I, sir. Indeed, I have not been in such an occasion before; and I make it a rule never to jest when I do anything for the first time. Come, draw, and put yourself in a posture of defence, or, by Heaven (so far as these two animals will allow me) I will make a mincemeat of you with my sword.

METRIS (*boiling over*). This is far more than any gentleman can endure! (*He stands before* BOUTROUX *with his left hand clenched behind his back, his right foot well advanced, and his sabre in tierce.*) Now, sir.

BOUTROUX (*very simply*). Now! (*Nothing happens.*)

METRIS. Sir, are you upon your guard?

On Anything

BOUTROUX. More or less (*jerking the horses*). Garrup! (*To* METRIS) Excuse me, sir, it seems that even in browsing grass this horse of mine has a devil of a hard mouth. He nearly sprained my wrist. . . . Well, then, are you upon your guard?

METRIS (*courteously*). I am.

BOUTROUX (*as in surprise*). Oh, you are! (*He gives a tremendous cut at the point of the neck, which his opponent skilfully parries and replies to by a thrust.*) Never . . . (*rapidly parrying a sharp succession of thrusts that follow from his opponent*) never . . . thrust . . . with a light cavalry sword. . . . I don't know much about (Ah, you missed that!)—much about . . . this business. But—— (*He suddenly gets round inside* METRIS' *guard, but has the misfortune to cut with a spent blow into nothing better than cloth. They disengage.*)

METRIS. Sir, you play well enough for a man who is uninstructed, but I warn you you are depending upon luck.

BOUTROUX. I know that. Luckily for me my mind is divided, and I can form no plan. For these animals at the end of the snaffle-rein have nearly pulled my arm off. However, let us have a second bout. The great thing for men like me is not to plan too much. (*Voices are heard through the fog.*) Sir, let me warn you like a gentleman, though my father is but a grocer, and yours for all I know a Rouge Dragon, that I hear the voice of one who is most indubitably my Colonel. And talking of *his*

226

The Fog

profession, he was, at the outbreak of this regrettable campaign, a butcher in Toulouse. He is a very brutal man, but I will not detain you, for your time is short.

METRIS. This is more than I will stand. (*They engage, and* METRIS, *whose blood is now up and who means business, gets* BOUTROUX *with a slash on the cheek at the third pass.*)

THE COLONEL (*now apparent through the thick fog, with a group of misty figures behind him*). Do I interrupt you, gentlemen?

BOUTROUX (*with great respect*). My Colonel, I had the misfortune to be separated from my troop during the fog, but I have taken this man (*pointing at the Austrian with his sword*) prisoner, but only after a sharp passage of arms, during which, my Colonel, I have been wounded. (*He points to the scratch on his cheek.*)

COLONEL (*coldly*). Lieutenant Boutroux, you shall have forty days. (*He turns to a soldier.*) Undo that scrimmage of bridles. (*The soldier obeys him. He turns to* METRIS *with great courtesy.*) I take it, sir, you are an officer in the forces of the Emperor and that you hold his commission?

METRIS. Undoubtedly.

COLONEL. Then, sir, you will follow me, for I take it you constitute yourself my prisoner. (*Turning to an officer upon his right.*) Major Clement, you will see to the enforcement of my sentence upon Lieutenant Boutroux. Pray add upon the record that he jested with a superior officer when discovered, separated from his command, fencing with a member of the enemy's forces. The Brigadier may deal with the complaint as he chooses.

BOUTROUX. Upon my soul, the longer I follow it, the less I comprehend the career of arms!

228

THE SPANIARD

WHEN I was in the French Army I met many men who had a constant tradition of the military past. These were not in the regiment, but one came across them in the garrison town where we were quartered, and among others there was an old man whose father had fought in the Peninsula and who retained a very vivid family memory of those wars. From this old man I gathered in particular what I had learned in general from reading, an impression of the Spaniard as a soldier, but that impression was false. It was false for many reasons, but chiefly for this: that Spain, like the United Kingdom, is very highly differentiated indeed, and province differs from province to an extent hardly ever grasped by those who have never visited the country.

When, many years later, I had the opportunity to visit Spain, this was the first point I noticed. It is particularly striking in the mountains. You will find yourself with one type of man talking Catalan in some small modern village; the way in which he tills his garden, the way in which his house is built, and the way in which he bargains with you, are all

On Anything

native to his race. You set off over the hills and
by evening you come to another village more different than is a Welsh village from an English one, for
you have crossed from Catalonia into Aragon.
Then, again, the boundary of the Basque Provinces,
or at least of the Basque race, is as clean as a cut
with a knife. One may argue indefinitely whether
this is because the Basques have preferred the
peculiar climate and soil of their inhabitance or
whether it is their energy and tenacity which have
changed the earth, but there it is. The Basque is
much more separate from the people around him
than is even (if he will pardon my saying so) the
Irishman of the West from the Scotchman of the
Lothians.

There is another form of differentiation in Spain
which is so striking that I hesitate for adjectives to
describe it lest those adjectives should seem excessive ; but I will say this, it is more striking than the
contrast between the oasis and the desert in Africa,
and that is pretty strong. I mean the differentiation produced by the sudden change from the high
plateaux to the sea-plains. The word " sea-plains "
is not strictly accurate, the belt running back from
the Mediterranean sometimes looks like a plain,
sometimes like an enclosed valley, more often it is a
system of terraces, hills upon hills, but at any rate
when you are once out of the influence of the sea
and on to the high plateaux which form, as it were,
the body of the Spanish square, you pass from

230

The Spaniard

luxuriance to sterility, from ease to hardship, and from the man who is always willing to smile to the stoic.

Then, again, you have the contrast between Andalusia and everything to the north of Andalusia. Andalusia was the very wealthy part of Spain under the Romans. It must always remain the very wealthy part of Spain so far as agriculture is concerned. It has easy communications and a climate like nothing on earth. Therefore, when the Moors came there they found a large, active, and instructed Christian population, and they ruined Andalusia less than any other part of Spain. Nay, in some odd (and not very pleasant) way they married the Asiatic to the European, and the European solidity, the European power over stone, the European sense of a straight line, were in Andalusia used by the vague imagination of the Asiatic to his own purpose, with marvellous results. All this has produced a quite distinct type of man ; and it is remarkable that, as is to be found in so many similar cases in Europe, the people exactly limitrophous to Andalusia on the north are peculiarly sparse, impoverished and alone. There lies the wide and arid sweep of La Mancha, imperishable in European letters.

Now, having said so much as to this high differentiation of the Spanish people (and one could add much more : the Asturias, always unconquered ; the Atlantic tides and rivers, the tideless Eastern harbours, the curious poverty of Estremadura ; the

On Anything

French experiments of Madrid and its neighbourhood, so utterly ill-fitted to the climate and the
genius of Spain), let me say something of the
Spanish unity.

No nation in Europe is so united. By which I do
not mean that no other nation is so homogeneous,
even in those deep things which escape superficial
differentiation. The Spaniard is united to the
Spaniard by the three most powerful bonds that can
bind man to man—religion, historical memory, isolation. It is not to be admitted by any careful
traveller that the religious emotion of the modern
Spaniard is either combative or profound. Indeed,
I know of nothing more remarkable than the passage
from Spanish to French thought in this respect.
You leave, let us say, Huesca; you notice at the morning Mass a moving and somewhat small concourse of
worshippers, few communicants, but above all in
the temper of the place, in the written stuff of the
somewhat belated newspapers, a sort of indifference;
as though the things of the soul " muddled through."
You bicycle a long day to Canfranc, the next day
you are over the hills (and Lord! what hills), and
there you are in the seething vat of the great
French quarrel. From the little villages right up to
the majestic capital, Toulouse, you feel the pulsation
increasing. Religion and its enemies are there at
war. The thing is vital, and men are quite ready to
die on either side. Of this, I say, you find little or
nothing in Spain; nevertheless, religion does bind

The Spaniard

the Spaniard to the Spaniard, and it binds him firmly to his kind. For the very fact that there is so little opposition, while it produces so much indifference, produces also a singular national contempt; and every man speaking to every other man knows with precision how that man's mind stands upon the ultimate things, how careless he is and yet how secure.

Again, the Spaniards are united by that profound historical memory which is a necessity to all nations and a peculiar asset in those who retain it alive. We in this country feel the appetite for an historical memory; we attempt to satisfy that appetite by the creation of legends; we call ourselves " Anglo-Saxons "—there is even, I believe, a notable body which will have us descended from the ten Lost Tribes. The French satisfy that appetite by recurrent experiences: the reign of the Grand Monarque, the Revolution, 1870. Glorious or tragic, each national experience gives a new impetus to the historic memory of the French people. Not so the Spaniard. All Spain is bound together by the enormous recollection of the Reconquista. Here is a province in which the Faith and the Roman Order were not recovered by persuasion (as was the case with Britain) nor were utterly lost (as was the case with Africa for so long) but were got back mile by mile as the prize of hard fighting. That fighting was, so to speak, the very trade of the Spaniards, from the time when Charlemagne was a little boy to the time when Henry VIII was a little boy. All the

story of our European growth, the time when we
were made, the time which is to the French the
accomplishment of their unity, to the English the
foundation of their institutions, to the Italians the
development of their art, that to the Spaniard is the
story of the Reconquista. And the Middle Ages,
which have impressed themselves upon every European nation as the glorious transition of youth impresses itself upon the sad memory of a man, stand
to the Spaniard for the Reconquista. This has
nothing to do with his knowledge of names or with
what is called "Education." It is in the blood.
The best proof of its result is this, that the Englishman invariably says of the Spaniard that, while other
nations show differences of manner changing from
class to class, the Spaniard is always a "gentleman."
The word "gentleman" is a very meagre word, but
on the whole the man who uses it best means the
tradition of the Middle Ages, and especially of the
fighting men which the Middle Ages produced, and
the Spaniard everywhere shows the external qualities
of those men. For instance, you cannot insult him
with impunity, and that characteristic, though we
often write it down, is one which in other nations is
somewhat rare. Take the modern for all in all, and
outside Spain, if you insult him he will usually argue.

Finally, the Spaniards are bound together by their
isolation. From the Straits of Gibraltar to the
Pyrenees, different as province is from province, you
feel everywhere something quite separate from that

The Spaniard

which lies north of the Pyrenees, and from the Pyrenees on, all over the west of Europe. Roads are an exception, paths the rule; the hours of meals, the very habit in the wearing of the clothes, the form of salutation, the mule taking the place of the horse, the perceptible restraint in every kind of converse, all these mark out the harsh soil which lends a perpetual note of nobility to the story of Europe. No man who has known Spain but would be able to say, if he were taken there blindfold, and suddenly shown his surroundings, " This is Spain." The frontier is sharp, the division clear, the isolation absolute.

The limits of these few pages forbid me a thousand things in this respect. I wish I could describe (for instance) how there is in every Spanish building, from the least to the greatest, something at once severe and strange. Bowling into that great harbour of Barcelona one sees the Customs House, a building with wings. Coming over the northern slopes of the Guadarrama one sees Segovia sailing out in some immortal way as though the cathedral and palace intended to attempt the air. Spain lives, and will revive by such imaginations.

It should be added, by way of closing these few notes, that the Spanish man is not only silent (which is perhaps a fault in him) but square, and so healthy in his limbs and in his mind that when he is rested and can speak again something will be changed in Europe.

THE FORTRESS

THERE is a province of Europe where a dead plain stretches out upon every side. It is not very extended if you judge by the map alone, it is perhaps but twenty-five or thirty miles from its centre to either of its boundary ranges; but to the eye it seems infinite, for it lies under that grey weather of the North in which the imagination exaggerates distance and so easily conceives imaginary flatnesses extending everywhere beyond the mist of the horizon.

In the midst of this plain there rises most abruptly a little market town. It stands upon a conical hill some 300 feet in height, and the impression it gives of being a rock or an island is enhanced by the height of its buildings, which, as is the case with nearly all mediæval work, are designed for a general effect, and are, whether consciously or unconsciously, as well planned and grouped as though one artist had sketched the whole and had left an inviolable design to posterity.

In this little town I had business some years ago to stop for the night, and when the next morning I found that there were two hours between my break-

The Fortress

fast and my train I walked out on to the crest of the
hill to see the view and to think about the past.   It
was autumn   the many artificially aligned trees
which bordered the winding, deserted avenues all
round the edge of the height were losing their
leaves; the air was singularly clear, and the effect
of the small but isolated height upon which one
stood was very strong.   I came to the north-eastern
corner of the huge ramparts which still surround the
little place, and there I found a most interesting
man.   He was upon the border between what are
called now-a-days middle age and old age; that is, he
was an old man, and if he lived would soon be a
very old man.   He was erect and spare; he was
short, and he had all the bearing of a man who has
been perpetually trained, and, indeed, I found out
when I got to know him better that he had seen
service in Africa and in Russia and in Mexico, three
very distant places.   He had never, however, risen
beyond the rank of colonel; he was a gunner, and
exceedingly poor, and he was finishing his life alone
in this little town.   They gave him meals at the
hotel for a sum agreed upon between them.   Where
he lodged he did not choose to tell me, but I fancy
in some very cheap and ruinous little room under
one of the big Flemish roofs of the place.   His only
pleasure was to take these walks about the town, to
read his newspaper before it was twenty-four hours
old, and to remember the trade in which he had been
engaged.

On Anything

We sat together on the very edge of the rampart, and I asked him, since it was his business to know so much about these things, whether the place would ever in his opinion enter once again into the scheme of European war.

He told me that this was absolutely certain; he said there was no field so small nor no village so forgotten, but in its cycle was swept by one or other of those armies which the peoples of Europe send out one against the other, pursuing various ends. This little town in which we sat had never seen an enemy for over two hundred years; yet there beneath us was the enormous evidence of its past. The trench was like a street fifty feet or sixty feet deep, as the house fronts of a street are, as wide at least as the narrow streets of any of these old towns, and on the further side the enormous heap of earth, and beyond it the level descent of the glacis. Here was a town not larger than some of our smaller English cathedral towns, Ely for instance, yet having round it such a mighty effort and proof of military determination as would to-day seem worthy of a great city. These fortifications ran all round the place, the two only gates in and out of it (through which ran the great road which linked the stronghold with the capital) were flanked by such works as the great modern forts occasionally show, and upon every point of its circumference one perceived the fixed will of a crushing Government responsible for all the destinies of a nation that this place should be inviolable.

The Fortress

My companion said to me : " Many men choose
many things as their examples of the way in which
nothing human can remain, and to most men the
best example is the change of taste in art or letters.
They point out how great buildings put up with infinite
care by men who loved them with all their souls
seem tawdry to an immediate posterity ; and they
wonder why verse which was supreme in their childhood is ridiculed in their old age. But to me the
most formidable proof of our futility is to be found in
works such as these. They succeed each other all
over Europe. Long before our written record began
you have the Cyclopæan Wars ; what you can see in
Tuscany and further east in the Mediterranean.
You have the Roman entrenchments, and the
mediæval castles, and the new system of Vauban
which the Italians created, and of which this earth-
quake before us is the finest work. And each in its
turn bears on into its future the stamp of futility.
Something changes in man : he makes a new weapon
(or he forgets the old), he develops a new method
of attack or a different mood in connection with war ;
nay, his very desires in the matter of victory change,
for he will desire in one generation glory, and in
another profit, and in a third the mere occupation of
a particular piece of sacred land. And as these
human things change in him, so the fortification of
his cities become like garments out of fashion and
are useless for their purpose and are thrown aside."

" You might then say," said I, " that those who

fortify to-day are foolish ; and, for that matter, you might add that those who have fortified in the past were foolish. For since each in turn is proved to be wrong with regard to the future, each generation might have spared itself this enormous labour."

" You are right when you call it enormous labour," said he, " but you are wrong when you say that it was ever futile. What a labour it is only those know who have looked closely into and meditated upon the fortifications of the past. The chalk hills and ramparts thrown up upon them by men perhaps who could use no spade and who depended for carriage upon baskets, which we to-day, when we estimate them in a modern method, reckon in fantastic sums of money; and this was done to defend, we know not what, by men every record of whom has perished. The ancient walls of the cities are much the largest and the strongest buildings they can boast, and much the most enduring. The transformation of a city two hundred years ago and more, when hardly a frontier place of Europe but had its elaborate system of main and out works, proves the same labour. Consider little Bayonne, never other than a little town, and yet flanked with a work which must have meant more than the building of a modern railway. And then, lastly, consider to-day the great garrisons circled with forts : Spezia and Metz, and the French frontier garrisons, and Antwerp and the line of the Meuse. And even, at the far ends of the world, Port Arthur, which, though it was never finished, was to have been among the greatest of all. Yes, it is a toil if you like, and that is why those who court defeat by boasting shirk it or ridicule it."

"But they are right to ridicule it," said I, "since time itself ridicules the walls of a city, and since it can be shown that no city has been made impregnable."

"You use a false argument," he insisted; "it is as though you were to say that because all men die therefore no man should live. These trenches and these walls and these circles of isolated forts to-day procure for men who fight under their shoulder a draft upon Time. That is what fortification is, and that is why all who have ever understood the art of war have fortified; and all who, upon the contrary, have in one way or another failed to understand the art of war, whether because they secretly desired to avoid arms or whether because they believed themselves invincible (which is the most unmilitary mood in the world!) have failed to fortify."

"I have heard it said," I answered him, "in the schools where such things are taught, that the Romans, as they were the chief masters of war, were also the most plodding in the use of the spade, and that not only would they fortify permanently every military post, but that they cast up a square field-work round them every night, wherever the army rested."

The little spare old gunner shrugged his shoulders. "They would have found it awkward," he said, "to do that in the case of a single battery quartered during manœuvres in a country house. But in general you are right: the Romans, who were the great masters of the art of war, thought of the spade and of the sword as of twin brothers, only the sword was the more noble, and in a fashion the elder of the two. At any rate, certainly those who are in the tradition of the Romans perpetually fortify. . . ." Then he asked me abruptly : " Since you are a foreigner and since you say that you have travelled (for I had told him of my travels when we made acquaintance), have you not noticed that wherever men are boastful or inept they despise fortifications, and that it is absent, and that the bases of their military action, their depots, their political centres, their harbours and dockyards lie open ? "

" I cannot tell," I answered, " for I have no knowledge of such things."

" Well, you find it is so," he said, and he walked away. He was much ruder and more long-winded than if he had been in the Cavalry, but you cannot have everything at once.

THE HUNTER

One day I had occasion to travel, at the expense of a fund more or less public, and certainly collective, in a railway train of which the carriages were *wagons-de-luxe*. It was by its description a train for the Very Rich, yet few of that numerous class were travelling in it, for it was going in the depth of winter from one of the most desolate highlands of Europe to another of Europe's most offensive deserts. I had business with one and the other.

There was in the dining-car of this luxurious train a gentleman who sat opposite me. He was dressed, as are so many of his class, in boots and striped trousers and a black coat and waistcoat. He had on a quiet tie of grey silk and what is called upon the Continent an English collar. He was nearly bald, but his eyes were determined, and his moustaches were of the shape and seemed to be of the size of buffalo's horns. They were of a metallic colour and looked like steel.

It is the custom on the Continent of Europe for males when they meet to accost each other, even if they have not been introduced, as indeed is the

243   R 2

custom (if you will observe it narrowly) of the mass of the population at home. There is, indeed, a story of a man who stood upon the bridge at Lyons wringing his hands and shouting out as he gazed upon the arrowy Rhone which was bearing down very rapidly a drowning human head : " Will no one introduce me to that gentleman that I may save him ? For I am an excellent swimmer." But this story would not apply to the mass of males upon the Continent. We therefore were ready to accost each other. He spoke to me in a curious language which I believed to be Hungarian—for though I do not know Basque I should have recognised the Basque terminations, and Finnish would not be used in the West of Europe, and save for Basque, Hungarian, and Finnish all other tongues have something in common. The Teutonic dialects, though they are infinite, can at once be distinguished, and a Russian does not address you in his own tongue in a foreign country. When, therefore, this stranger man had spoken to me in this tongue which I believed to be Hungarian, I replied to him gently in the Limousin dialect as being the most southern with which I had any acquaintance, and upon the principle, that with foreigners the more southern you are the better chance you have. He answered in pure Italian, which is of no use to me. I spoke to him then in the French of Paris, which he understood ill, but did not speak at all. At last we tumbled upon a mutual language, which, for the honour I bear you,

The Hunter

I will not name ; but it was neither Latin nor Arabic,
nor the language of the Genoese ; and if I called it
lingua franca you would feel a legitimate annoyance.

We had not spoken of many things before he told
me his own characteristics, which were these : that
he was a brave man but modest ; that he had a contempt for riches, and was content to live upon the
small income derivable from funds inherited from
his father ; that he revered the memory of his
father ; that he was devoted to his mother, who
lived in a modest way in a provincial town, hating
the extravagance of the capital.   He further told me
that he had been by profession a soldier, and upon
my asking whether his stoical life were not diversified
by some amusement he answered that he had permitted himself certain recreations, but only those
befitting the uniform he wore, and notably was he
addicted to the chase of wild and powerful beasts.

"It is often remarked," he said, "by those who
know nothing of the business, that modern firearms
have made the destruction of the larger carnivora too
easy a task for the sportsman.   This may in general
be the case, but only if men are fighting under
luxurious conditions.   A man going out by himself
with his gun, unaccompanied by a dog, and determined
upon the destruction of some one considerable four-
footed beast of prey, still runs a certain risk."

"You are right," said I, "and a relative of mine
who under such conditions attempted the bear,

though having only designed to attempt wild-fowl, in the impenetrable thickets of Scandinavia, was very bitterly disappointed and has been lamed for life."

At this my companion was a little put out. "The bear is not carnivorous," he said, "and a brave man should be able to tackle a bear with his hands. I really cannot understand how your relative (as you call him), if he had a fowling-piece or even so much as a pocket-pistol with a range of ten yards, could not shoot off a bear. . . . But to return to my original thesis, which is that the larger carnivora are really dangerous to a man walking alone, however well armed he may be. It was so armed but undefended by companions that I found myself on the borders of the Indian Ocean five years ago . . ."

"Which border of that vast sea did you inhabit?" said I with some curiosity, and I was beginning to make a list of all its boundaries, including the magnificent but undeveloped districts which fringe the north-west of the great island of Australia, when he went on as though I had not spoken—

". . . A tiger, or, I should rather say, a tigress, growled in the dense underwood, and I was immediately upon the alert."

"Knowledge," I replied, "is a remarkable thing; it amazes me and my friends who are familiar with the classics, though I believe there is very little to know in that department. Even the chemists astonish me, and the people who talk technically about warships are remarkable men; but I see that in your case, as in that of so many others, I have

The Hunter

more to learn with every day I live, for there came a
growl from the underwood and you knew it to be
that of a tiger—nay, of a tigress. But," I continued,
lifting my hand as he would interrupt me, "though
it fills me with admiration it does not make me
hesitate, for I know men who can talk a language
after passing a week in the country to which it is
native, and I beg you to fulfil my curiosity."

"I heard the growl of a tigress," said he, eager
to continue his narrative, "proceeding from the
underwood, which is called in that country *rawak*."

"Why is it called *rawak?*" I interrupted.

"Because," he explained, with an intelligent look,
"it is composed of *mera* roots and *sinchu* closely
interlaced, with a screen of reeds ten feet high or
more waving above it."

I told him that I now perfectly understood and
desired to hear more.

"I heard," said he, "the growl of a tigress, and I at
once made ready my arm and prepared for the worst."

"When you say made ready your arm" (I again
interrupted him) "I want to seize the matter clearly,
for the interest of your tale absorbs me—what exactly
did you do to the instrument, for I am acquainted
with a certain number of firearms, and each has to
be prepared in a different manner?"

"I pulled the bolt," said he coldly, and then
maintained rather an offended silence.

"Did you not snap the safety catch?" said I, in
some fear that I had put him out by my cross-
examination.

On Anything

" No, sir," said he, " my rifle (for such it was) was adorned by no such appliance. But I pulled the spring ratchet home. And by way of precaution I pressed my thumb upon the main-pin for fear that the ratchet of the cambor should slip from the second groove."

" Now I understand you perfectly," I said, " and I beg you to continue." And as I said this I leaned my head upon my hand so far as the jolting of the express train would allow me, and watched him with a thoughtful frown.

" Well, sir," went on the Unknown in an independent manner, " if you will believe me, when the beast sprang I missed him—I mean her."

" One moment," I said, " one moment. I cannot believe you. You mean that you missed some vital spot. That you missed so enormous an animal in mid-air, as large as a cottage, and in full career to bear you down, fraught with death, with pain, and with defeat, spreading its arms like windmills, and roaring to announce its approach—that I will not believe."

" You are right," said he, eyeing me in an iron manner, "I did not wholly miss the ferocious monster —or rather, monstress. When we sportsmen say ' miss' we mean hitting some part of the animal which is not vital or which still permits it to pursue its abominable purpose. At any rate the tigress (for such it was) fell to earth within a few feet of me. It did not reach me. It had miscalculated its spring. . . ."

The Hunter

"It is a curious point," said I (always desirous to pursue a conversation and to prolong it), "how difficult it is for a man, or a beast for that matter, to estimate the distance which he has to jump. I well remember trying to jump the River Rother, which is near the eastern boundary of my own county. . . ."

"You will allow me," he interrupted.

"No, sir," I continued, "pray let me tell you what I had to say, for it is in my mind and I wish to be rid of it. I well remember, I say, trying to jump the River Rother and missing by three feet, but if you will believe me——"

"Will you allow me?" he said, a little angrily.

"In a moment, sir," said I, "in a moment. . . . Well, I say I missed it by three feet, and many a friend of mine has missed things by a little minus, but the funny thing is that they never miss it by a little plus. Now, isn't that worth judging? I did indeed know one case . . ."

"I am determined you shall allow me," said my companion, becoming earnest.

"One moment," I pleaded, lifting my right hand slightly from the table. "I was once with a man who had to jump from an old piece of fortification on to the top of a wall about ten feet off, and if he jumped not far enough he fell into the soft ditch about five feet deep. But if he jumped too far he fell into an enormous fosse a hundred feet deep. And, by the Lord, he jumped exactly three inches too far! Poor devil! . . . Now, if this tigress of

249

yours had only jumped just over your head you
would have had her at a disadvantage. You could
have changed your front with the rapidity familiar
to men of your profession, organised a concentrated
fire against her just as she was executing her turning
movement, and got her behind the shoulder-blade.
But . . ."

"There is no 'but,'" said he, with an impressive
but rather dangerous solemnity. "I say that the
tigress came to earth just in front of me and advanced
upon me by one and by two. I had no time to reload
and to fire. I was all alone. What did I do?"

"That is what I was waiting to hear," I said.
"It seems to me the climax of the whole story. I
trust that you seized its—or I should say her—upper
jaw with your left hand, lower jaw with your right
hand, and tore the head asunder. There is no
quicker way with a tigress."

"You are wrong," said he.

"Did you not, then," said I, "suddenly fasten
both hands upon its throat and, digging your thumbs
conversely from right and from left upon its wind-
pipe, strangle it to death? Such a manœuvre is a
matter of moments, and he laughs best who laughs
last."

"I did not," said he, in a rising anger.

At this moment the train began to slow down,
and I knew the place it was approaching, for I am
very familiar with the line. A porter who did not
know me, but whom I secretly bribed, perceiving
the danger of the circumstances, took my bag and

The Hunter

made a great noise with it and asked a number of questions. Everybody got up, and the crowd of us began to jostle down the gangway of the eating-car. The Hero was at first just behind me, and was beginning to explain to me what exactly he did to the tigress when we were unfortunately separated by two commercial travellers, a professional singer, and a politician.

Fate dominates the lives of men, though Will is a corrective of Fate. Men in a restaurant-car are like the leaves that flutter from trees or like the particles of water in the eddying of a river. I drifted from him further and further still. When we came out upon the crowded platform I saw him, the Hero, waving his hand to me, desiring to re-establish with me human and communicable things and to tell me how he did at last destroy that mighty beast. But Fate, which is the master of human things, would not have it so, and Will, which is but a corrective of Fate for us poor humans, stood me in no stead. We drifted apart; we never met again. He was off perhaps to shoot (and miss) some other tigress (or, who knows, a tiger?) and I to another town where I might yet again wonder at the complexity of the world and the justice of God!

Anyhow, I never understood how he killed the tigress. Were it not for the evidence of my senses I should be willing to believe that the tigress killed him. But we must never believe anything that is even apparently against the evidence of our senses.

Farewell, dear mortals!

OUR INHERITANCE

How noble is our inheritance. The more one thinks of it the more suffused with pleasure one's mind becomes; for the inheritance of a man living in this country is not one of this sort or of that sort, but of all sorts. It is, indeed, a necessary condition for the enjoyment of that inheritance that a man should be free, and we have really so muddled things that very many men in England are not free, for they have either to suffer a gross denial of mere opportunity—I mean they cannot even leave their town for any distance—or they are so persecuted by the insecurity of their lives that they have no room for looking at the world, but if an Englishman is free what an inheritance he has to enjoy!

It is the fashion of great nations to insist upon some part of their inheritance, their military memories, or their letters, or their religion, or some other thing. But in modern Europe, as it seems to me, three or four of the great nations can play upon many such titles to joy as upon an instrument. For a man in Italy, or England, or France, or Spain, if he is weary of the manifold literature of his own

252

Our Inheritance

country can turn to its endurance under arms (in which respect, by the way, victory and defeat are of little account), or if he is weary of these military things, or thinks the too continued contemplation of them hurtful to the State (as it often is, for it goes to the head like wine), he can consider the great minds which his nation has produced, and which give glory to his nation not so much because they are great as because they are national. Then, again, he can consider the landscapes of his own land, whether peaceably, as do older men, or in a riot of enthusiasm as do all younger men who see England in the midst of exercising their bodies, as it says in the Song of the Man who Bicycled:

> . . . . and her distance and her sea.
> Here is wealth that has no measure,
> All wide England is my treasure,
> Park and Close and private pleasure:
> All her hills were made for me.

Then he can poke about the cities, and any one of them might occupy him almost for a lifetime. Hereford, for instance. I know of nothing in Europe like the Norman work of Hereford or Ludlow, where you will perpetually find new things, or Leominster just below, or Ledbury just below that again; and the inn at each of these three places is called The Feathers.

Then a man may be pleased to consider the recorded history of this country, and to inform the fields he knows with the past and with the actions of

men long dead. In this way he can use a battlefield
with no danger of any detestable insolence or vulgar
civilian ways, for the interest in a battlefield, if it is
closely studied, becames so keen and hot that it
burns away all foolish violence, and you will soon
find if you study this sort of terrain closely that you
forget on which side your sympathies fail or succeed :
an excellent corrective if, as it should be with
healthy men, your sympathies too often warp
evidence and blind you. On this account also one
should always suspect the accuracy of military
history when it betrays sneering or crowing, because,
in the first place, that is a very unmilitary way of
looking at battles, and, in the second place, it argues
that the historian has not properly gone into all his
details. If he had he would have been much too
interested in such questions as the measurement of
ranges, or, latterly, the presence and nature of cover
to bother about crowing or sneering.

When a man tires of these there is left to him the
music of his country, by which I mean the tunes.
These he can sing to himself as he goes along, and
if ever he tires of that there is the victuals and the
drink, which, if he has travelled, he may compare to
their advantage over those of any other land. But
they must be national. Let him take no pleasure in
things cooked in a foreign way. There was a man
some time ago, in attempting to discover whose
name I have spent too much energy, who wrote a
most admirable essay upon cold beef and pickles,
remarking that these two elements of English life

Our Inheritance

are retreating as it were into the strongholds where England is still holding out against the dirty cosmopolitan mud which threatens every country to-day. He traced the retreat of cold beef and pickles eastward towards the City from the West End all along Piccadilly and the Strand right into Fleet-street, where, he said, they were keeping their positions manfully. They stand also isolated and besieged in one hundred happy English country towns. . . .

The trouble about writing an article like this is that one wanders about: it is also the pleasure of it. The limits or trammels to an article like this are that, by a recent and very dangerous superstition, the printed truth is punishable at law, and all one's memories of a thousand places upon the Icknield Way, the Stane Street, the Pilgrim's Way, the Rivers Ouse (all three of them), the Cornish Road, the Black Mountain, Ferry Side, the Three Rivers, all the Pennines, all the Cheviots, all the Cotswolds, all the Mendips, all the Chilterns, all the Malvern Hills, and all the Downs—to speak of but a few— must be memories of praise—by order of the Court. One may not blame: therefore I say nothing of Northwich.

.   .   .   .

Some men say that whereas wealth can be accumulated and left to others when we die, this sort of inheritance can not, and that the great pleasure a man took in his own land and the very many ways in which he found that pleasure and his increase in that pleasure as his life proceeded, all die with him.

On Anything

This you will very often hear deplored. As noble a woman as ever lived in London used to say, speaking of her father (and she also is dead), that all she valued in him died with him, although he had left her a considerable fortune. By which she meant that not only in losing him she had lost a rooted human affection and had suffered what all must suffer, because there is a doom upon us, but that those particular things in which he was particularly favoured had gone away for ever. His power over other languages and over his own language, his vast knowledge of his own county, his acquired courtesy and humour, all mellowed by the world and time, these, she said, were altogether gone. And to us of a younger generation it was her work to lament that we should never know what had once been in England. Among others she vastly admired the first Duke of Wellington, and said that he was tall— which was absurd. Now this noble woman, it seems to me, was in error, for all of us who have loved and enjoyed know not only that we carry something with us elsewhere (as we are bound to believe), but leave also in some manner which I do not clearly perceive a legacy to our own people. We take with us that of which Peter Wanderwide spoke when he said or rather sang these lines—

> If all that I have loved and seen
>   Be with me on the Judgment Day,
> I shall be saved the crowd between
>   From Satan and his foul array.

Our Inheritance

We carry it with us. And though it is not a virtue it is half a virtue, and when we go down in the grave like the character in *Everyman*, there will go down with us, I think, not only Good Deeds, a severe female, but also a merry little hobbling comrade who winks and grins and keeps just behind her so that he shall not be noticed and driven away. This little fellow will also speak for us, I think, and he is the Pleasure we took in this jolly world.

But I say that not only do we carry something with us, but that we leave something also; and this has been best put, I think, by the poet Ronsard when he was dying, who said, if I have rightly translated him, this—

"Of all those vanities" (he is speaking of the things of this world), "the loveliest and most praiseworthy is glory—fame. No one of my time has been so filled with it as I; I have lived in it and loved and triumphed in it through time past, and now I leave it to my country to garner and possess it after I shall die. So do I go away from my own place as satiated with the glory of this world as I am hungry and all longing for that of God."

That is very good. It would be very difficult to put it better, and if you complain that here Ronsard was only talking of fame or glory, why, I can tell you that the pleasure one takes in one's country is of the same stuff as fame. So true is this that the two commonly go together, and that those become most glorious who have most enjoyed their own land.

THE NEW ROAD

IT is at once the most amusing and the most dramatic feature of our time that we can foresee—for some few years ahead—material things. Things moral escape us altogether. Never was there a generation of Europeans who could less determine what the near future held for the fate of national characters, of religions, or of styles in art ; the more foolish attempt to escape this ignorance by pretending that things moral depend upon things material. They observe the cutting of a canal and prophesy the decline of one nation upon its completion, the growth of another—as though the power of nations armed resided in something lower than the Mind, and as though the success of armies (upon which all at last depends) were determined by the exchange of metals or by new routes of trade. Meanwhile, though the future, even the immediate future, of nations and of faiths is more closely hidden from us than ever, yet it is entertaining, and, as I have said, it is even dramatic, to watch our power of prophecy over material things.

We undertake works of such magnitude and spread

The New Road

over so long a span of years, they are accomplished under such conditions of international comprehension and security, that we can stand (sometimes) in a desert place and say, " Here, in five years, will be a town," or on a barren coast and say, " Here, in five years, will be a harbour." We can distract ourselves by imagining the contrast beforehand and by return-ing, when the work is done, to see how nearly one has imagined the truth. Bizerta once afforded such an opportunity, Rosyth now affords one, and so does that sight which set me writing this, and which I have just witnessed in a remote and hitherto quite silent valley. There, with little advertisement of public interest, one of the immemorial high-roads of Europe is under restoration and is about to return to life : the old High Road into Spain.

It is often remarked that the lines of European travel can hardly be permanently altered, that Nature has designed them. Generations do sometimes pass in which some profound change in man rather than in Nature affects a few of the great roads. The Roman line from the south northward, the highway from the Saone to the Straits of Dover, passing by Laon and Amiens, was deflected as the Dark Ages closed round the mind of Gaul. Water carriage succeeded the degraded high-roads. The conver-gence of water-ways in the basin of Paris made that basin the centre of travel, and the old way by Laon was forgotten. Yet modern conditions restored it. The railway has done again what the Roman engineers accomplished, and Laon is once again a halt upon the great road southwards, and once again the most direct avenue from the Channel to the Mediterranean follows the plain to the east of Paris. So it has come to be with a road equally famous, equally forgotten, the High Road from the North into Spain.

The Pyrenees lie, as every one knows, like an artificial wall between the valley of the Ebro and Gaul. How great the division is only those can believe who have seen with their own eyes the meadows and the deep orchards of Bearn, and then, after a painful crossing of the hills, have come upon the burnt deserts of Aragon. The road from the one to the other, the administrative road which bound Spain to Gaul, which connected Cæsaraugusta with Tolosa, that is, Saragossa with Toulouse, was Roman Highway, called "the High Pyrenean," the highest and most central of the two main passes. It had, as I have said, Toulouse for its northern terminus, Saragossa for its southern. It had for two mountain towns, or depots, at the foot of either climb, Oloron, the town of the Ilurones, on the north; on the south the Bishop's town of Jaca. It had for its last outpost just before the last steep Urdos, the Forum Ligneum, to the north; to the south a cluster of huts and a station, whose Roman name has not come down to us, but which since the barbarian invasions has been called "Canfranc." This great road, like so many throughout the Empire, fell. You may yet trace its

The New Road

structure in those places where it is not identical with the modern way, but with the close of the Empire, and on nearly to our own time its surface was left unrepaired. Armies used it, as they used all the great Roman roads of the north and west, till the Twelfth Century. The Merovingians crossed it in their raids to the Ebro; Charlemagne sent men down it in the advance upon (and failure before) Saragossa—the expedition whose retreat was clinched by the destruction of his rearguard and the death of Roland in Roncesvalles. It was still a gate for armies when the reconquest of Spain from the Mohammedan began. Jaca was free before any other town of the Central North, Huesca fell before the first Crusade was fought, Saragossa before the second. Bearn, and indeed all Christendom, still used that high notch until the new civilisation of the Middle Ages had set in with the Twelfth Century, but from that beginning till our own time it was more and more forgotten. Spain, reconquered, corresponded with Europe by the sea. The two land roads that bound the Peninsula to Christendom ran round either end of the Pyrenean Chain. The central pass was abandoned when the great development of French roads, which was the work of Louis XIV, was imitated—most imperfectly—by his grandson in Madrid, it was the road by Burgos, Vittoria, and Bayonne that was renewed; the commercial energy of the Catalans in the same generation opened the Perthuis, broke into the Roussillon, and connected

On Anything

Barcelona with Perpignan and with Narbonne. But Aragon, the pivot and centre of the old Reconquest, Saragossa, the main town of the Roman communication with the north, lay off the two tracks of travel, half forgot Europe and by Europe were ill-remembered. It was Napoleon, or, to be more accurate, the Revolutionary Crusade, which reopened the central pass, and here, as in so many other places, began the return to Roman things. While the armies of the Empire, with their train and their artillery, were still tied to the sea road from the Roussillon, a small force without guns passed up the old Roman road (now come to be called the "Somport"), marched over its silent grasses, wading the Arroyos, the bridges over which had long since fallen in, appeared suddenly before Jaca, occupied that citadel, and pursued the way to Saragossa, there to join the main army and to lay a siege memorable beyond all modern sieges for an heroic defence. Buonaparte seized the advantage of that passage. He desired a road over which artillery could go. It was one of twenty which he so desired over the mountain ranges of Europe, and which a full century has barely seen completed; for within four years of his resolution his supremacy was broken at Leipsic and destroyed at Waterloo. The Third Empire continued the tradition; the road was carried up on the French side of the pass, but the universal power of 1808 was gone and the Spanish approach was neglected. It was not till the other

The New Road

day, till our own generation, that the full work was
done, and that the great street from Toulouse to
Saragossa right over the hills was once more open
to the full power of travel. Yet travel failed it. In
the meanwhile the railways had come; they had
followed the coast roads, and the main line from
Madrid to Paris ran tortuously through the mountains
of Castile and turned twenty times in the labyrinth
of Basque Valleys, between Vittoria and Irun.
Saragossa was still upon one side; Aragon still
remained remote; the new road was empty beneath
the cliffs of its great hills.

To all this exception in Europe I had grown so
used that I took pleasure, during each of my yearly
passages over this road, in noting its loneliness, and
in considering how the noise of this chief way
between the south and the north had been silenced
for so many centuries. The absence of men and of
public knowledge was a perpetual, a renewed, and a
permanent curiosity. There are many sites in Europe
once peopled now lonely, once famous and now
ignored, but this place seemed to be especially
eccentric, and to have passed from something which
had long been like the Æmilian Way or the stages
of the Rhone Valley to something as untouched as
the uplands of Cheviot or the moors of the West
Riding over Ribble and above Airedale—very lonely
places.

This year I found that the last change had come.
Far down the Gave d'Aspe, in the gorge where

On Anything

Abdurrahman led the Mohammedan invasion into Gaul, there came loud thunders, for all the world as though it were really thundering on the gloomy shoulders of Anie, so many thousand feet beyond the clouds. Then, as I neared the head of the vale I saw Man at it. He was at it in swarms. He had dammed the torrent; he had fixed great turbine tubes, and he had begun the Hole in the Hill. For just the few miles of the ridge itself there was still silence—as there is still silence above the Gothard on the high road—but up from the Spanish valley, rolling up from it as it had rolled down the Val d'Aspe, came again the human thunder, and when the road had fallen its two thousand feet and touched the water of the River Aragon, there again was Man in great numbers working like an ant, burrowing under the terrible Garganta and determined upon his Hole in the Hill. The two tunnels will meet when each has accomplished three or four miles, and the work will be done. There will be a straight way from Paris to Madrid; the Pyrenees will have lost their unbroken line; the Roman scheme will have re-arisen; Saragossa will come forward again into the list of great European cities, and people will hear of Aragon. I do not know whether to be glad—seeing such proof that Europe always returns to itself—or sorry.

ON TWO TOWNS

THE wide countrysides of Europe sum themselves
up in central cities : municipalities inheriting from
Rome. The lesser towns group round the larger;
the bishops of the lesser suffragan to metropolitan
of the greater cities, as it was fixed in the Roman
order which Constantine inherited from Diocletian
and which everywhere stamps the West with the
framework of the Fourth Century. These great
cities are not only the heads and inspirers of their
provinces, they are also the gathering places of
armies ; the contrast and the fellowship between
them is especially seen when either is the capital of
a wide plain below a mountain range. Then each
becomes the depot and the goal in turn of invading
forces, each stands for the national fortunes upon
either side of the passes. So, for the great Alps,
you have Augsburg and Milan ; so for the Vosges,
Strasburg and Nancy ; so for the Pyrenees, Saragossa
and Toulouse.

No two cities in Europe are more representative
of their provinces or stand better for symbolising the
nature of their land. From the towers of each the

long line of the Pyrenees may be traced, especially
in early autumn mornings when the sky is clear with
the approaching cold and when the first snow has
fallen upon the summits. From Toulouse the dark
Northern escarpment runs along the southern horizon
in a wall, surprisingly level and seeming tiny in its
long stretch or belt of grey; from Saragossa, much
further off and more rarely the white strips and
patches can be caught behind the nearer foothills,
the whole in a glare of sunlight full upon it, like a
desert tilted up; you just see them over dry, treeless
plains, and immediately the sun rises they are lost in
the hot haze. The Pyrenees thus stand between the
two cities and belong to each, and the legends of
the mountain regard now one, now the other, or, as
in the Song of Roland, both combined (for the Horn
of Roland as he died was heard southward in Saragossa, northward in Toulouse), and the smoke of each
may just be seen or guessed from certain heights,
from passes that look southward into Aragon or
northward into Aquitaine.

Alone of the central bishoprics of these hills they
are united by a road, and have so been united for two
thousand years. Characteristically, in the true spirit
of the Pyrenees, there is but that one great road
between them. It takes men, and has taken them
since the legions made it, up by Huesca and Jaca
and so over the Summus Pyrenæus, the " Somsport,"
then down by the deep valley of Bearn to Oloron, to
Pau, to Tarbes, and down the river bank to Toulouse.

On Two Towns

All the armies have taken it. Through this paved gap went the first Frankish kings, still wild, wandering South for spoil, and through it in a tide poured the Mohammedan host that so nearly seized upon Europe. All such marchings brought up under the walls of one or other of the cities: Saragossa for ever besieged from the North, Toulouse beating off the raids from the South, fight similar wars. Each has its river, and the river of each is the life of the two provinces on either slope of the mountains; the Ebro of Aragon, the Garonne of Aquitaine. Each has its port: the one Barcelona, the other Bordeaux; and in each valley there is separation of thought and custom—something like hostility—between the inland city and the commerce of the sea. Each was for long the centre of a nation, each afforded the title of a great house. Aragon was built up under its princes, from that remote age when the chieftain of a few mountain clans began to fight his way South against the infidels till the light grew strong upon the Twelfth Century and Alphonso fixed himself and the Faith upon the Ebro. Toulouse grew under its counts to be almost a nation, ruling everything from the Cevennes to the Pyrenees, and making a rallying place, schools, law courts, and an imperial middle for all the fields of the Garonne.

So far the parallel between these twin cities holds; but the test of any appreciation of them is contrast.

The landscape of Saragossa is a baked plain, ill-watered and reflecting up to heaven the fierce sun of

On Anything

Spain like a plate of bronze. The landscape of Toulouse is of fields and meadows with many trees. The Ebro trickles under the great bridge of Saragossa for weeks together; then perhaps dies altogether, becoming rather a stagnant pool or two than a river; then, in spate, rises high and threatens the piles, roaring against them, and suddenly sinks again. The Garonne runs in a broad, even stream, shallow, but full and never lacking water; it is already placid as it sweeps under the great bridge of Toulouse. Saragossa became the capital of a true kingdom whose language, traditions, and above all whose chivalrous aristocracy were its own. Toulouse went under in the false adventure of the Albigensian schism. Saragossa was Mohammedan, a sort of northern bastion of Islam, till far into the development of the Middle Ages: it did not re-enter Christendom till 1118. The First Crusade was long past, England was all Norman, while yet this city was governed by Asiatic ideas in contempt of Europe. Toulouse, always Christian, rose against the unity of Christendom. Saragossa in those struggles got a great hero and his legend, a man who fighting now for Islam and now for us built up an epic, the Cid Campeador, the "Challenger." Toulouse has no heroes. Saragossa became a pivot of steadfast faith, round which turned and on which reposed the reconquest of Spain by men of our race. Toulouse was— and to-day still is—perpetually seeking new things and divergence in Europe: a sort of smouldering fire. To-day full of denials of things sacred yesterday, dogma, the family, property, all the foundations. Saragossa lies indifferent, ready to become (as it is becoming) more wealthy and careless of these philosophical quarrels.

The great churches of the two towns are in violent contrast too. At Toulouse these are all of one pattern and old. The place where St. Saturninus, the evangelist of the city, died—the church of the "Toro," the Bull (for a bull dragged him to death through the streets of the city)—is of small Roman brick, plain, steadfast. The vast cathedral to which his body was translated is of that same brick, and all the arches are Roman, round and small. The Dominican Church is the same; a stranger sometimes takes one for the other. In Saragossa the cathedral is stamped with the fervour of the reconquest. It is crammed with detail and with infinite carving. It is very dark, high and silent, and at the same time, with its wealth of creation and of figures, magical. Toulouse has no monument of faith other than those similar early simple and huge temples. Saragossa has the colour, the tinsel, and the gorgeousness of the late Renaissance in the gilded Basilica of the Pilar.

Religion, which is at once the maker and the expression of States, differs utterly in mood between one city and the other. In Toulouse there is war. The men who deny and the men who affirm are at it with all the weapons of our time, as six hundred years ago they were at it with swords. You buy a newspaper, and ten to one the leading article will be an affirmation or a denial of the creed—signed by some famous name. In Saragossa you may buy newspapers for a month and get nothing but the common news, two days old. Mass is crammed at Toulouse, empty in Saragossa. There are enemies of the Mass in power at Toulouse, numerous, vigilant, convinced. In Saragossa a few eccentrics or none. Toulouse would persecute one way or the other had it a power separate from the State. Saragossa was always tolerant; of its few murders one was the popular murder of an Inquisitor. There is something that sleeps in Saragossa for all its liveliness and wealth and air. There is something that wakes and prowls in Toulouse for all its ancient walls and green things growing upon ruins as they grew in Rome.

These are the two cities as I know them. Often upon a height upon the Pyrenees I have thought how one lay beneath me to the left, the other to the right, the end of a chance journey. All human tracks from the mountains seem to lead down like water-courses to one or the other place, and travel flows of its own weight to the sunlit market-place of Saragossa or to the Capitol of Toulouse from every saddle in the hills. You may be in the Cerdagne (which is Catalan) or in Roncesvalles (which is Basque), but if you are on foot and wish to go far the roads will bring you insensibly to the great

town on the Ebro; you may be as far west as St.
Jean-Pied-de-Port or as far east as Ax, but on the
northern slope insensibly you will be driven to
Toulouse. The two cities are the reservoirs of life
on either slope of the hills, and each holds, as it
were, a number of threads, which are paths and
roads radiating out to the high crossings of the
chain.

And, as I consider the two towns, whether near
them as I lately was or here at home, I find almost
as great a pleasure in imagining their future as in
remembering their long past and the sharp picture
of their present time. The Provinces of Europe
develop, but they do not change their identity. If
it be paradoxical to suggest a wealthy Saragossa and
a fanatical Toulouse, yet it is not out of keeping
with the revolutions of Europe. Saragossa is on the
road to wealth in a country which is rapidly accumu-
lating; Toulouse is well on the road to fanaticism
and religious war. One can see Toulouse with great
artists and fierce rhetoric standing out against some
reaction of thought in the Republic or captured by
the flame that has set fire to Lourdes; one can see
Saragossa dragged into the orbit of Barcelona,
drifting with the rising wealth of Mediterranean
commerce, forgetting altars, and sharing the mere
opulence of the Catalans. Such thought leads one
to fantastic guesses; it is provoked by the modern
character of these two great, unwritten, ill-known
Pyrenean towns in one of which the chief quarrel of

On Anything

our time is so actively pursued, in the other of which lies all the new promise of Spain.   And that reminds me.   Saragossa has no song of its own ; Toulouse has one called " If the Garonne had only wished, she might. "

So much for Saragossa and Toulouse.

THE JUDGMENT OF
ROBESPIERRE

" IT is of little profit," said Robespierre severely,
" that we should debate what may or may not come
to pass in that time. You speak of more than a
hundred years, and of a season when the youngest
child before us shall have long been dead, and his
child, too, perhaps be dead after him ; and for that
matter, even if it profited us, it would not be to the
service of God, for we must say what is true and
defend it. As for the rest, no man is master of
destiny."

He was about to make an allusion to the people of
Epirus and to a discovery of theirs which he had
read in the classics upon this subject, when St. Just
interrupted, as was his way, with burning eyes and a
sort of high, rhetorical facility which gave all his
young words such amazing power. He was sitting
in an attitude one might have thought listless, so
lightly did his delicate hand lean upon his knee,
save that all thought of carelessness left one when
one watched the intensity of his face. And he
repeated a phrase which its rhythm has made famous,

On Anything

"The things we have said will never be lost on earth."

It was in the weeks after Fleurus. Charlotte Robespierre, ill-tempered and silent, sat like a sort of guardian of the room upon the little sofa by the western wall of it, the darkest side. Couthon was there, the cripple, his face permanently stretched by pain, and there also, almost foreign—English or Italian one might have said from their length— shone the delicate features of Fouché, his thin lips firm and inevitably ironical.

Paris was glorious. There was a festivity in the sky of that July, a cool air in the sunlit streets, and that sort of clear sound which comes up from the gulfs of the narrow ways when Paris in summer is at the full of its life. The sunlight upon the courtyard shone reflected from the white walls of it into the darkness of the little room where the friends sat talking together before they should go down to the Parliament. In the shed outside was the noise of their host, the carpenter, sawing. A very quiet and respectful young man, the son of the house and secretary to Robespierre, ventured an opinion. He had a wooden leg and his expression was not intelligent. When these two generations of men had passed, he said, the Goddess Liberty would be firm upon her throne. It would be the chief advantage of the passage of time that men would forget all the old days of slavery, and that the evil thing which the Revolution was occupied in destroying would be

274

remembered only as a sort of nightmare of humanity. The insolent palaces which might remind men of their tyrants will have been pulled down long ago, and their gew-gaws of pictures have been left to moulder. He foresaw and was about to describe at some length the reign of Virtue and Equality among men, when Robespierre interrupted him severely in his high voice and bade him not to pirouette upon the stump of his wooden leg, which wore the carpet of the Citizen his father, and was, moreover, an ungainly gesture. He further told him with increased severity that the arts in a State of free men would always be decently cherished, for but a few weeks before he had been delighted to sit for his portrait to M. Greuze.

There was a little silence following this reprimand.

" If it be of any moment to you," he continued, " I can, I think, tell you some things certainly that society will hold. For they have invariably accompanied liberty in her majestic march. Men will respect the labour and the property of others, and the power of peace and war will reside with the people. It is to this," he added earnestly, " that I have given my chief efforts, and I believe I have placed it upon a secure foundation. What I am most afraid of," he mused, " is the power that may be put into the hands of representatives. But that again will be tamed by long usage. I shall soon see to it that the places of meeting are made largely public, and I have drafted a design whereby it shall

On Anything

be death, or at least exile, to plan so much as a municipal building for the meetings of municipal bodies unless the galleries permit a full view of the debate, and accommodate a number of citizens not less than five times the total number of the elected. It would be better," he sighed in conclusion, "that a law should compel at intervals great meetings in the open, and should punish by the loss of civic power all those who did not attend, unless, indeed, they had been given leave of absence by some magistrate."

St. Just was weary of the war, and asked him how long it would continue.

"It will continue," said Robespierre firmly, and in the tone of a man who can speak more definitely of near things than of distant, "it will continue until the winter at least, upon which occasion I design . . ."

At this point Charlotte, whose temper was not improved by such discourses, abruptly left them. They heard the sharp hurrying of her footsteps cross the flags of the courtyard; she was going up to her own room overlooking the street. Fouché smiled.

"You smile, Fouché," said Robespierre, displaying very obvious irritation, "because you think, as politicians do, that war is an unaccountable thing. Let me tell you that reason here is much stronger than chance, and that the forces opposed to us are already convinced of liberty. I have before me" (he pulled out his little brown book from his pocket) "a list of pamphlets recently distributed beyond the frontiers, and a very good estimate of the numbers of their readers."

Fouché restrained his smile; he was a man capable of self-control to any limit. He leant his long, delicate, refined head upon the tapering fingers of his left hand, and listened with great apparent interest to what the Master was saying. The sawing in the courtyard without ceased, and his host, the carpenter, entered in that reverential way which marks the sentiment of religion, and very silently took a distant chair to listen to the Master's discourse. Couthon shifted himself in his place to relieve his crippled members, and Robespierre continued—

" Nothing endures unless it be based upon Virtue, but though Virtue tends to corrupt with time, and though Liberty is rather for what the fanatics have called 'angels' than for men, yet if men's chains are broken it has great chance of permanence and of effect upon the public. I have upon this matter," he continued, pulling out of a pocket a shagreen case and from that case a pair of spectacles, " certain notes that will not be without interest for you.'

Fouché sighed while Robespierre was seeking among a group of neatly-folded papers for what he had to read. His host, the carpenter, bent forward to hear as a man might bend forward to hear the reading of the Gospel. He even had an odd instinct to stand up and listen with bowed head. St. Just was thinking of other things. And certainly any modern man looking on would have been compelled to watch St. Just's deep and luminous eyes. He had already forgotten the future, and once again he was thinking of the wars. He had begun to take pleasure in the charges. A moment might have made him, from the poet that he was, a soldier; and while the high thin voice of the little man Robespierre went on with appropriate gestures, describing the permanence of Virtue in a free State, he clearly saw what he had seen but a few days before from the lines : the houses of the beleaguered city against the June dawn, and he heard the bugles.

Robespierre had begun : " The sentiment of property which is native in man proceeds from what he gives to Nature by his toil, and this is respected by all, yet even property itself cannot be thought secure until Virtue be there to guarantee it, no laws can make up for its absence. It is Virtue, therefore, upon which even this essential, without which society cannot be, reposes. And Virtue which will cause a poor man to be equal with the rich, while the one regards the other without envy upon the one side, without contempt upon the other."

For a full quarter of an hour Robespierre went on, and Couthon, as a matter of ritual, and the master of the house as a matter of religion, listened : the one as a matter of course, the other ardently. And when he had finished his little peroration, when he had taken off those spectacles and wiped them, when he had turned upon them his pale, small, watchful, grey-green eyes, he noted that Fouché alone had been inconstant. Fouché had his back turned and was looking out of a window. A boy who passed through the courtyard whistling, carrying a short ladder, looked at the window for a moment and saw the aquiline, refined face covered with laughter. The boy thought that laughter merely friendly. He waved his hand and smiled an answer, and Fouché saw in that boy the generation that should arise. He composed his features and turned them once more towards the room. Before Robespierre could speak sharply, as he meant to speak, and complain of such inattention, he said in a clear, well-modulated voice, that he had never heard those sentences before. Was Robespierre to pronounce them that day in Parliament?

"I shall do so," said Robespierre, "if I am permitted by the President to speak. If not, I will reserve my remarks for another occasion." He pulled out a fat little round watch prettily enamelled, touched the lace at his wrists, settled the order of his stock, and said as a schoolmaster might say it to young St Just: "Are you not coming with me?"

St. Just, startled suddenly like a man awakened, thought of the hour, remembered the Parliament, and went out with his friend.

Fouché with his hand to his chin crossed the courtyard and went up the stairs to that part of the

On Anything

house which overlooked the Rue St. Honoré. He had something to say to Charlotte. Couthon, who was hungry, remained to lunch, but he found his hosts dull and a little ill-tempered. He could not fill the void that had been left by Robespierre